SpringerBriefs in Philosophy

SpringerBriefs present concise summaries of cutting-edge research and practical applications across a wide spectrum of fields. Featuring compact volumes of 50 to 125 pages, the series covers a range of content from professional to academic. Typical topics might include:

- A timely report of state-of-the art analytical techniques
- A bridge between new research results, as published in journal articles, and a contextual literature review
- A snapshot of a hot or emerging topic
- An in-depth case study or clinical example
- A presentation of core concepts that students must understand in order to make independent contributions

SpringerBriefs in Philosophy cover a broad range of philosophical fields including: Philosophy of Science, Logic, Non-Western Thinking and Western Philosophy. We also consider biographies, full or partial, of key thinkers and pioneers.

SpringerBriefs are characterized by fast, global electronic dissemination, standard publishing contracts, standardized manuscript preparation and formatting guidelines, and expedited production schedules. Both solicited and unsolicited manuscripts are considered for publication in the SpringerBriefs in Philosophy series. Potential authors are warmly invited to complete and submit the Briefs Author Proposal form. All projects will be submitted to editorial review by external advisors.

SpringerBriefs are characterized by expedited production schedules with the aim for publication 8 to 12 weeks after acceptance and fast, global electronic dissemination through our online platform SpringerLink. The standard concise author contracts guarantee that

- an individual ISBN is assigned to each manuscript
- each manuscript is copyrighted in the name of the author
- the author retains the right to post the pre-publication version on his/her website or that of his/her institution.

Erika Ruonakoski

Sisters of the Brotherhood: Alienation and Inclusion in Learning Philosophy

Erika Ruonakoski
Department of Social Sciences
and Philosophy
University of Jyväskylä
Jyväskylä, Finland

ISSN 2211-4548 ISSN 2211-4556 (electronic)
SpringerBriefs in Philosophy
ISBN 978-3-031-16669-3 ISBN 978-3-031-16670-9 (eBook)
https://doi.org/10.1007/978-3-031-16670-9

© The Author(s) 2023. This book is an open access publication.
Open Access This book is licensed under the terms of the Creative Commons Attribution 4.0 International License (http://creativecommons.org/licenses/by/4.0/), which permits use, sharing, adaptation, distribution and reproduction in any medium or format, as long as you give appropriate credit to the original author(s) and the source, provide a link to the Creative Commons license and indicate if changes were made.
The images or other third party material in this book are included in the book's Creative Commons license, unless indicated otherwise in a credit line to the material. If material is not included in the book's Creative Commons license and your intended use is not permitted by statutory regulation or exceeds the permitted use, you will need to obtain permission directly from the copyright holder.
The use of general descriptive names, registered names, trademarks, service marks, etc. in this publication does not imply, even in the absence of a specific statement, that such names are exempt from the relevant protective laws and regulations and therefore free for general use.
The publisher, the authors, and the editors are safe to assume that the advice and information in this book are believed to be true and accurate at the date of publication. Neither the publisher nor the authors or the editors give a warranty, expressed or implied, with respect to the material contained herein or for any errors or omissions that may have been made. The publisher remains neutral with regard to jurisdictional claims in published maps and institutional affiliations.

This Springer imprint is published by the registered company Springer Nature Switzerland AG
The registered company address is: Gewerbestrasse 11, 6330 Cham, Switzerland

Acknowledgements

This publication was written as the intellectual output of the Erasmus+ Strategic Partnership, Gender and Philosophy, initiated by Sigridur Thorgeirsdottir (University of Iceland, coordinating university), Martina Reuter (University of Jyväskylä), Tove Pettersen (University of Oslo) and Antje Gimmler (University of Aalborg). These philosophers formed the project's academic board and developed the original idea of the book, as well as planning the content and teaching of the related summer schools, which were held in each country in 2016–2017. The exchange between the board members and myself guided my writing process in its early stages, and I am particularly grateful for their comments on the manuscript. During the project, I shared my office with Reuter at the University of Jyväskylä, which resulted in numerous discussions on the work in progress and joint involvement in various events. What is more, Reuter's previous work on the underrepresentation of women in philosophy laid the groundwork for the questionnaires we prepared to gather data about students' experiences of learning philosophy.

I am also indebted to Thorgeirsdottir and Eyja Margrét Brynjarsdóttir for inviting me to the Feminist Utopias conference in Reykjavík and Skálholt in the spring of 2017. This extremely inspiring conference allowed me to get feedback about our project and to discuss it with researchers who shared similar interests. I am equally thankful to Elsa Haraldsdóttir for taking such excellent care of the numerous practicalities of the project, and, above all, for being such a trustworthy friend in our shared adventures during the summer schools.

On behalf of the project I would also like to thank Óskar E. Óskarsson from the Icelandic Centre for Research for making our Erasmus+strategic partnership run smoothly and Pia Søndergaard for diligently arranging the practicalities at the University of Oslo. In addition, I wish to thank all the visiting lecturers of the summer schools: Virpi Lehtinen, Donata Schoeller, Ásta Sveinsdóttir and Charlotte Witt, who taught in Reykjavík; Sandrine Bergès, Marguerite Deslauriers and Sara Heinämaa, who taught in Jyväskylä; Henrik Jøker Bjerre, Robin May Schott, Ole Ravn and Pauline Stoltz who taught in Aalborg; and finally, Sarah Clark Miller and Anna Smajdor, who taught in Oslo.

During one of the most intense work periods pertaining to this book, I spent 3 weeks in Olot, Catalonia, in the autumn of 2017, invited to the Faber Residency during its special theme of feminism. I thank the director of the residency programme, Francesc Serés, for his hospitality and friendliness, and my co-residents Sameena Azhar, Bipasha Baruah, Mary Condren, Jenn Diáz, Kate Good, Susie Hammond, Raisa Jurva, Kathleen McNerney, Viktoriia Panova, Klara Regnö, Fina Sanz, Marta Roqueta and L. Ayu Saraswati for the inspiring conversations we had during our residency. I am also grateful for the intellectual exchange and walks I was able to have with yet another co-resident, the author Patricia de Souza, who unfortunately passed away only a couple of years after our residency.

Auli Dahlström, whose group I belonged to during my pedagogical studies, opened up for me a new dimension in thinking about teaching and learning. Margaret A. Simons, with her warmth and genuine interest in others, regardless of their academic rank, has taught me more about generosity than perhaps any other individual. Tua Korhonen reminded me to exercise caution with claims about ancient Greek texts and helped me to analyse the background of a particular passage attributed to Phintys. In addition, my philosopher colleagues in Helsinki and Jyväskylä, Saara Hacklin, Anniina Leiviskä, Olli-Pekka Moisio and Jussi Saarinen, have been helpful when discussing my ideas pertaining to the book. I particularly want to thank Martta Heikkilä, Susanna Lindberg, Irina Poleshchuk and Janne Vanhanen for commenting on the chapter "The Historical Situation" in our seminar and for helping me to see the whole manuscript with fresh eyes. Sanna Tirkkonen has generously shared her views on good and inclusive practices of teaching philosophy, whereas a sound walk organised by Vanhanen inspired a part of my discussion pertaining to embodiment in learning processes. Likewise, the support and interest of doctoral and postdoctoral researchers such as Olli Aho, Heidi Elmgren, Tiia-Mari Hovila, Sari Hietamäki, Olli-Pekka Paananen, Milla Rantanen, Jaakko Vuori and Minna-Kerttu Vienola have been important to me.

In 2017–2022, I had the opportunity to present my work in several occasions, including the Philosophy Research Seminar and Genders through Time conference at the University of Jyväskylä, and Silent History—Women Philosophers in Finland, an event organised by the Finnish Society for the History of Science and Learning, Philosophical Society of Finland and Association for Women and Feminist Philosophers in Finland. I am extremely grateful for all the discussions we had on those occasions and for the participants' comments, and I particularly want to thank Ella Kemppi and Markku Roinila for their input in the organisation of the latter event. I am likewise grateful to the active members of the Centre for Practical Phenomenology, with whom I have been able to try alternative ways of arranging scholarly events in the field of philosophy.

Most of all, I wish to express my gratitude to all the students of the Gender and Philosophy summer schools, as well as to all my students at the University of Jyväskylä, for sharing their views with me and for the experience of learning together. I hope that you will find some of your concerns covered in this work and that it can, perhaps, inspire you in your own teaching practices in the future. I also want to thank my family: my husband Juhani and our sons Rainer, Väinö and Joel. Juhani has most often been the first to learn about the twists and turns in the writing process. His attentiveness and encouragement have been an invaluable support to me.

The writing of this book was for the most part funded by the Erasmus+programme of the European Union. The extensions of my contract by the Department of Social Sciences and Philosophy (University of Jyväskylä) made it possible for me to delve into this project more profoundly, and for this, I am grateful to Heinämaa, Mika Ojakangas, Reuter and Mikko Yrjönsuuri. The finishing touches to the manuscript were put during my projects *Despair and Time* and *Indirect Philosophy as a Form of Resistance*, which both enjoyed the generous funding of the Kone Foundation. I would like to thank all the involved individuals and organisations for their support, without which the finishing of this book would not have been possible.

Contents

1 Introduction: Equality, Inclusion and Alienation in Learning Philosophy 1
  1.1 Why Does the Underrepresentation of Women in Philosophy Matter? 1
  1.2 Data on the Underrepresentation of Women in Philosophy 4
  1.3 Sexual Harassment and Gender-Based Harassment 7
  1.4 Subtle Mechanisms of Discrimination: Implicit Bias, Micro-Inequities and Stereotype Threat 10
  1.5 The Structure of the Book 13
  References 16

2 Undoing Power Hierarchies 19
  2.1 Feminist Pedagogy 19
  2.2 Gender and Philosophy Summer Schools 23
  2.3 Concepts of "Situation" and "Alienation" 24
  References 26

3 The Historical Situation 29
  3.1 The Historical Roots of Women's Inclusion and Alienation in Philosophy 29
  3.2 The Perpetuation of Women's Marginality 32
  3.3 Dealing with the Tradition: Intimacy and Idolatry 34
  3.4 Why and How to Raise Awareness of Early Women Philosophers ... 41
  3.5 The Jyväskylä Summer School: Feminist Thinking in Historical Perspective 44
  References 46

4 The Affective, Social and Bodily Situation 49
  4.1 Women Students' Passion for and Alienation from Philosophy 49
  4.2 Class, Race and Sexual Orientation 56
  4.3 Further Reflections on Embodiment 61
  4.4 The Reykjavík Summer School: Nature, Emotions and the Body ... 64

	4.5 The Aalborg Summer School: Feminist Political Philosophy and Problem-Based Learning	66
	References	69
5	**The Moral Situation: Self and Other**	73
	5.1 Power Struggles in the Classroom and How to Move Beyond Them	73
	5.2 Recognition, Generosity and Care	78
	5.3 The Oslo Summer School: Care Ethics and Conflicts	81
	References	84
6	**Conclusions and Further Questions**	87
	6.1 General Conclusions	87
	6.2 Questions to Ask Oneself	89
	6.3 Philosophy and the Politics of Education: What's Next?	91
	References	94
Index		95

Abbreviations

AP   *Anthologia Palatina* (*The Palatine Anthology*, *The Greek Anthology*)
DL   Diogenes Laertius, *Lives of Eminent Philosophers*
NE   Aristotle, *Nicomachean Ethics*
Rep. Plato, *The Republic*

Chapter 1
Introduction: Equality, Inclusion and Alienation in Learning Philosophy

Abstract When we are talk about the underrepresentation of women in philosophy, what do we mean, and what kind of data do we have on it? Why is the low percentage of women and other minorities in philosophy a problem? Are there specific mechanisms of discrimination that contribute to women and minorities opting out of philosophy?

1.1 Why Does the Underrepresentation of Women in Philosophy Matter?

Over the past decade, professional women philosophers have increasingly voiced their discontent and disappointment about the persistent underrepresentation of women and racial, ethnic and gender minorities in the field of philosophy. This concern stretches much further into history, and the underrepresentation itself is as old as Western philosophy. In our days, the underrepresentation of women and other minorities still encompasses all levels of academic philosophy, from students to those involved in teaching.

When this concern is raised, this immediately begs the question whether it matters how many women practise philosophy. After all, opting out and choosing another field may be wise, as far as economic possibilities and even emotional rewards are concerned. What is more, we witness a similar disproportion in many other fields, such as nursing or engineering, without necessarily thinking twice about it. It is possible to argue, however, that a more even gender distribution could be for the good of the development of even these fields: diversity as such can be seen as beneficial, as it can bring new questions with it, or different ways of looking at familiar questions. Would not philosophy also benefit from attracting more students with diverse gender identities, as well as from different ethnic and economic backgrounds? Is it possible that the homogeneity of the staff and student body leaves philosophy outside many of the developments that enrich the rest of the humanities? This is the justification of what is beneficial for philosophy itself (see e.g. Friedman 2013, 32–36). Even if

© The Author(s) 2023
E. Ruonakoski, *Sisters of the Brotherhood: Alienation and Inclusion in Learning Philosophy*, SpringerBriefs in Philosophy,
https://doi.org/10.1007/978-3-031-16670-9_1

groups were underrepresented because their members have more interesting study paths to follow, we can still regret this absence as a loss to the discipline of philosophy.

Another justification points towards what is beneficial to women and minorities themselves. Learning philosophy can be beneficial to the currently underrepresented groups in a number of ways: (1) it can be highly enjoyable, (2) it develops the student's capacity for critical in-depth analysis, and (3) as professional philosophers, women and members of other minorities can take part in the analysis and development of philosophical approaches rather than just apply them. Such participation implies, in turn, intellectual and social influence.

Finally, and perhaps most self-evidently, we can ask what is just towards women and other minorities in philosophy. It is hard to question the justness of creating a learning and working environment in which nobody feels alienated because of their gender, sexual orientation, ethnicity, race or social background. If the absence of such an environment is one reason for the underrepresentation of women and other minorities, then one can consider the current state of affairs as unsatisfactory and requiring change. What is more, an organisation that claims to be committed to justice and equality is simply inconsistent, if it allows unjust structures to persist.

A great deal has already been written on the topic of women's underrepresentation in philosophy. For the most part, the discussion deals with the situation of professional women philosophers in the academic community. Linda Alcoff's *Singing in the Fire: Stories of Women in Philosophy* (2003) is a collection of women philosophers' reminiscences of the problems they have faced in their careers. Katrina Hutchison's and Fiona Jenkins's (eds) (2013) *Women in Philosophy: What Needs to Change?* discusses widely the situation of women in philosophy, with a detailed analysis of the gendered aspects of implicit bias, stereotype threat and microinequities. Michael Brownstein's and Jessica Saul's (eds) *Implicit Bias and Philosophy*, volumes 1 and 2, (2016a, b) investigate the psychological and ethical aspects of implicit bias in philosophy, covering, for instance, the themes of rationality, knowledge, structural injustice and moral responsibility. Among the numerous articles that deal with the problem of discrimination and the essentialist tendencies of some approaches to women's situation in philosophy, we can mention Louise Antony's "Different Voices or Perfect Storm: Why Are There So Few Women in Philosophy?" (2012) and Anne Leuschner's "Why So Low? On Indirect Effects of Gender Bias in Philosophy" (2019). Helen Beebee's and Jennifer Saul's report *Women in Philosophy in the UK* (2011) and its recent update (2021) are, in turn, significant and compact resources for statistics, actions, initiatives and recommendable practices. In addition to these publications, a number of empirical surveys on women's underrepresentation in philosophy majors have come out in the past years (see Sect. 1.2).

As all of these publications demonstrate in their own way, women's underrepresentation in professional philosophy is intertwined with the learning and teaching of philosophy. In the remainder of this introduction, I discuss the data provided by empirical research as well as some of the viewpoints suggested by analytic philosophers to deal with the issue of underrepresentation. The overall focus of this volume, however, is not on professional women philosophers but on where the seeds of the issue are sown, in the situations faced by women students of philosophy and in the pedagogical responses to the potentially alienating elements in those situations.

The concepts of "situation" and "alienation" are the most central to my discussion of women students' marginal position in philosophy (see Sect. 2.3). There appears to be something in the practice and public image of philosophy that is experienced as more alienating by the underrepresented groups than by most of the White—and supposedly heterosexual—males, who form the overwhelming majority of students and staff. The goal of the study is to identify the sources of alienation on the basis of earlier empirical and philosophical research, and to examine how teaching and learning practices could contribute to making philosophy more welcoming towards women and other minorities, as well as towards those who belong to the White and male majority but still experience a similar alienation.

The title of the book, *Sisters of the Brotherhood: Alienation and Inclusion in Learning Philosophy*, refers to the situation of women as both included in and alienated from the male-dominated field of philosophy, as well as to inclusive practices in philosophy teaching. In other words, my focus is on women, even though I consider race, class and other possible sources of students' alienation from philosophy. Despite the fact that philosophy as a discipline is now much more welcoming towards women than it was, for instance, in the 1960s (see Simons and Ruonakoski 2021), their situation is still different from that of men, according to whose interests and social styles the practices of the philosophical community have been formed over its long history.

Some attempts have already been made to improve the situation of women and other minorities in philosophy. Different countries and universities have taken different measures, which makes assessment of the overall situation difficult: some have renewed their policies on hiring practices, others are focusing on the inclusiveness of the syllabus, and so on. Recommendations that advance gender parity are extremely important, of course, and one of the book's objectives is precisely to identify the relevant non-discriminatory practices that can be implemented at the departmental level. An equally important objective, however, is to help readers recognise that the other's experience always remains hidden from the view of the explorative philosophical gaze—not only in its immediacy but also in its singular situatedness. Consequently, the problems I am able identify may differ from those seen by a person who has a different background—for instance, a different gender identity, sexual orientation, ethnicity or social class. In fact, the problems of the other can be invisible to me simply because I never encounter our "shared" environment in the way that the other does. The volume therefore advocates the recognition of one's "not-knowing" as an important ethical and pedagogical goal, one that allows change to go deeper than the level of administrational necessity, which is often adhered to only half-heartedly. In this spirit, I hope to appeal to the imagination of those of us who teach philosophy, especially in higher education, and to provide some tools that might help readers analyse the power dynamics in the classroom. I also suggest ways in which the diversity of students could be addressed in the teaching of philosophy.

The motivation of this volume being practical in the described sense, I have taken the liberty to integrate discussions from different theoretical perspectives in it: phenomenology, analytic philosophy, empirical research and psychoanalytic theory.

As background research for the book, a small-scale survey on students' experiences of studying philosophy was conducted, and interviews were made with a number of philosophy students and professionals of philosophy from various countries (see Chap. 4). The book incorporates many pedagogical ideas of the philosophers who designed and organised the experimental summer schools in the Gender and Philosophy project. While the discussion on the summer schools and their pedagogical input is necessarily coloured by my own pedagogical leanings, there remains a certain polyphony in these sections that hopefully enriches the work. As for the interviews and survey, I have likewise wanted to highlight opinions that are not necessarily identical with my own, but help us get a broader understanding of possible ways of interpreting the aspect of gender in philosophy.

Questioning the styles of interaction in learning and teaching philosophy inevitably leads to questions about the nature of philosophy itself. What are the aspects of philosophy that we find valuable and worth preserving, and what are those that we should, perhaps, dispense with, to make room for more inclusive practices of philosophy? What is the future of philosophy like? How do we actively create this future—or is it enough to carry on the tradition? These questions are, of course, without unequivocal answers, but at the same time relevant to all practitioners of philosophy, whether or not they engage in teaching.

All in all, I have approached the question of learning and teaching philosophy by investigating the philosophical basis of that learning and teaching. While the volume at hand includes practical pedagogical suggestions and guidelines, I have written it as a philosopher who invites fellow philosophers to investigate the question of gender and pedagogical choices in all their complexity. That the topic is approached predominantly from the viewpoint of existential phenomenology is perhaps most visible in how the themes of situatedness, temporality, intersubjectivity and embodiment are treated in the book, as well as in the chosen concepts. I elucidate the power relations in the learning environment and demonstrate how women and men come to occupy different possibilities in a seemingly egalitarian setting. Drawing from Simone de Beauvoir's vision of the development of gender, I discuss the different aspects of situations of students and the teaching staff. In addition, I examine the formation of alienation from philosophy among students, suggesting that their experiences of belonging and alienation are formed in a complex process in which philosophy is never "pure" but always structured in a historical and social context. In the following section, I consider underrepresentation from the viewpoint of empirical research, returning to more general pedagogical and conceptual questions in Chap. 2.

1.2 Data on the Underrepresentation of Women in Philosophy

For most people working in the field of philosophy today, the underrepresentation of women and other minorities in it should be evident. When one peeks into a classroom

1.2 Data on the Underrepresentation of Women in Philosophy

or a meeting room of a philosophy department or participates in a conference, it is not unusual to witness what looks like an overwhelming preponderance of White male students. During the past decade, quite a few empirical studies dealing with the issue have emerged. The data comes primarily from the English-speaking countries, and problematically, does not allow direct comparison even between those. In the British data, we can see a steady decline in the proportion of women from the undergraduate students (46%), the graduate students (37%) and PhD students (31%) to staff members with temporary (28%) and permanent jobs (24%) (Beebee and Saul 2011, 8). The figures from Australia tell us that while in 2001–2008 as many as 61% of students taking introductory courses in philosophy were women, only 44% of those graduating with a philosophy major and 41% of those with a PhD were women (Bishop et al. 2013, 235–236). These figures still seem rather high in comparison to the UK, but among staff, the tendency is similar: in 2009, women comprised only 28% of the faculty (Bishop et al. 2013, 232).

Some quantitative studies have been conducted on gender parity in philosophy in the United States (e.g. Paxton et al. 2012; see Bishop et al. 2013, 246). However, the low percentage of respondents makes it difficult to generalise the results. For this reason, I only refer to a result obtained at the University of Oklahoma by Heather Demarest et al.: on introductory courses to philosophy, women are 51% of students, but in more advanced courses, only 37% of students. In 2003, the proportion of women in full-time philosophy faculty positions was only 17% (Demarest et al. 2017, 525).

These trends are indicative of the situation in the Nordic countries, even though no large-scale study has been done (see, however, Reuter 2015). Generally speaking, philosophy differs significantly from the other humanities that tend to be female-dominated, and more closely resembles mathematics, physics and engineering in that all of these fields are male-dominated. Across different countries and universities there is a significant drop in the percentage of women students between introductory courses and more advanced ones. This result is often interpreted as indicative of a possibility to foster gender balance by how philosophy is taught.

In an American study, Morgan Thompson et al. (2016) examined the possible motivators of women's opting out. They looked into seven different aspects of this: (1) identification with philosophy, (2) perceived instructor fairness, (3) perceived student respect, (4) comfort of speaking in class, (6) beliefs about field-specific ability and (7) beliefs about gender and race gap. One of their findings was that the students' perception of the proportion of women on the syllabus had an influence on whether women were willing to continue in philosophy or not. (Thompson et al. 2016, 16.) Even though the results remain fairly inconclusive overall, the researchers argue that there is a significant difference in how women and men experience their belonging to the field, to the disadvantage of women. As for methods of teaching and learning, Thompson et al. (2016, 18) suggest that women are less likely to enjoy thought experiments as a method of practising philosophy, and that therefore a wider variety of teaching methods could be of use to attract more women students to major in philosophy. In addition, highlighting the relevance of philosophy to a wider range of problems might make it more interesting to women.

A similar result is obtained by Demarest et al. (2017). The researchers argue that two attitudes predict continuation in philosophy, namely "feeling similar to the kinds of people who become philosophers" and "enjoying thinking about philosophical puzzles and issues" (Demarest et al. 2017, 526–527). Women are less likely to hold these attitudes than men. The researchers suggest that having more women instructors or more women authors on the syllabus may not be the only way to tackle the issue of "feeling similar", for at least in some cases it may be enough to point out the counter-stereotypical characteristics of a historical philosopher to make room for diversity and to provide objects of identification. As for enjoying "philosophical puzzles and issues", women were less likely than men to hold this attitude in the beginning of an introductory course, but the likelihood to do so dropped even lower during the term. (Ibid., 529–531.)

As the researchers admit (Demarest et al. 2017, 530), the way they formulated the question was somewhat problematic, because the emphasis on "philosophical puzzles" reinforces the idea of philosophy as a game that works through thought experiments. In other words, the formulation directs the respondents' attention to a specific mode of practising philosophy. However, in an environment in which philosophy is practised mainly in a manner that detaches it from the everyday concerns and works with thought experiments, a low interest in "philosophical puzzles" can understandably predict discontinuation.

In their survey on women's opting out from philosophy at the University of Sydney, Dougherty and others found that there may be pre-university factors that have an effect on women's low likelihood to identify themselves with the discipline. According to them, a gender schema may be operating that is very difficult to undo by increasing the number of female lecturers (I use "lecturer" here as a concise term for university teaching staff) or making changes in the teaching methods. However, the researchers point out that women's choices of disciplines should be examined on a larger scale, because they do not choose between philosophy and nothing, but philosophy and other disciplines, many of which apparently fascinate a good part of women students more than philosophy does (Dougherty et al. 2015, 471; see also Reuter 2015, 16–17).

In another study, Debbie Ma et al. (2017) demonstrate that women are more likely than men to view the discipline as masculine and less likely to identify with it, and that there is a correlation between these two things: the women who think that philosophy is "a masculine field" have difficulties identifying with it. Male students' perception of the field as masculine, however, does not correlate with their likelihood to continue in philosophy. In contrast to Dougherty et al., Ma et al. suggest that it is possible to influence the gender disparity in philosophy through a pedagogy that does not reinforce the view of philosophy as a masculine discipline.

Without a doubt, there are many other variables that may have an effect on women students opting out of studying philosophy. Experiences of philosophy (if any) while in upper secondary school, the public image of philosophy and even the location of the university are likely to have an impact.[1] For instance, 50% of the applicants accepted to study moral philosophy at the University of Helsinki were women in 2016, when students still started directly as majors in a specific subject.[2] At the same time, a smaller Finnish university further from the capital, the University of Jyväskylä, had a significantly lower percentage of accepted women applicants (12%) and a yet lower percentage of women applicants in philosophy all in all, regardless of the fact that its emphasis in the history of philosophy, phenomenology and critical theory might be considered more attractive to women than the focus on analytic philosophy at the University of Helsinki. This suggests that the location of the university may play a role. Before the reasons behind these differences are investigated empirically, it is anybody's guess whether they can be explained by the quality of teaching of philosophy in upper secondary school in different areas, by women's preference for more secure choices in education outside the metropolitan area, by the metropolitan area's attractiveness to women, or by something else. In any case, the impact of location cannot alone explain the general underrepresentation of women in philosophy. Especially when students choose their major only after taking introductory courses in several subjects, the actual teaching of philosophy at the university level and the ways of interacting in the classroom will have more influence on students' choices.

1.3 Sexual Harassment and Gender-Based Harassment

During the past few years, there has been a lot of discussion about harassment and discrimination within philosophy.[3] This discussion preceded the second and more

---

[1] Whether philosophy is an obligatory subject in upper secondary school and its equivalents varies from one European country to another. French and Finnish students of upper secondary school (*lycée*, *lukio*) are expected to learn philosophy, whereas in the UK, for instance, it is optional.

[2] This information can be found in the database of the Statistics Finland, the Ministry of Culture and Education and the Finnish National Agency for Education. https://vipunen.fi/en-gb/university/Pages/Hakeneet-ja-hyväksytyt.aspx. Accessed 19 April 2022.).

[3] For instance, the blog *What Is It Like to Be a Woman in Philosophy?* collects and publishes the recollections of harassment and discrimination experienced by women students and members of faculty. https://beingawomaninphilosophy.wordpress.com. Accessed 31 March 2022. The reported incidents range from situations, in which women's input is ignored, to sexual assaults. The blog currently has a sister blog *What We're Doing About What It's Like*, which deals with the institutional and individual responses to problems for women in philosophy. https://whatweredoingaboutwhatitslike.wordpress.com. Accessed 31 March 2022.

global rise of the #MeToo movement in 2017,[4] which, within a very short time, radically changed not only the debate on sexual harassment but on the way gender relations are addressed and understood, and how all forms of harassment are dealt with.[5] What is more, in the years following the rise of the #MeToo movement more research has been done on sexual harassment in academia. The movement has certainly had its impact within philosophy, adding to the ongoing discussion of gender relations and harassment in the field and making it, perhaps, at least a bit easier for students and faculty to speak up about harassment.

How should sexual harassment and gender-based harassment be defined? In EU Directive 2002/73/EC sexual harassment is defined as a situation "where any form of unwanted verbal, non-verbal or physical conduct of a sexual nature occurs, with the purpose or effect of violating the dignity of a person, in particular when creating an intimidating, hostile, degrading, humiliating or offensive environment". How the specific acts of sexual harassment are defined varies from one country to another. According to the Finnish Equality Act, for instance, sexual harassment can be expressed by "sexually suggestive gestures or expressions, indecent talk, puns and comments or questions referring to body parts, clothing or private life, pornographic material, sexually suggestive letters, emails, text messages or phone calls, physical contact, suggestions or demands for sexual intercourse or other kinds of sexual activity, rape or attempted rape".[6]

Gender-based harassment is defined in the Finnish Equality Act as "unwanted contact that is not of a sexual nature but which is related to the gender of a person, their gender identity or gender expression, and by which the person's psychological or physical integrity is intentionally or factually violated and an intimidating, hostile, degrading, humiliating or offensive atmosphere is created". Gender-based harassment is expressed by "degrading the individual's gender, gender identity or gender expression", or by "workplace and school bullying, when this is based on the victim's gender".[7] However, it is important to see that in an American consensus study report by National Academies of Sciences, Engineering and Medicine (NASEM), for instance, gender-based harassment is defined as one form of sexual harassment, the other two being unwanted sexual attention and sexual coercion (NASEM 2018, 48).

Legislation gives its own answers to how sexual harassment should be understood, but how individuals in different countries understand it does not necessarily

---

[4] As it is well known, the #MeToo movement was initiated in 2006 by Tarana Burke to empower sexually assaulted women of colour through empathy. The idea was to post the words "me too" on social media to support assaulted women. In 2017, Alyssa Milano reintroduced the concept as a way raise consciousness of the magnitude of the problem of sexual harassment.

[5] Most importantly, it has become less stigmatising for victims of sexual harassment and assault to speak out. At the same time, the #MeToo movement has been criticised of reaffirming the idea of gender as binary and women as victims.

[6] See the Finnish Act on Equality between Women and Men, Equality Act, 27. https://julkaisut.valtioneuvosto.fi/bitstream/handle/10024/75131/Act_on%20Equality_between_women_and_men_2015_FINAL.pdf?sequence=1. Accessed 31 March 2022.).

[7] Ibid.

1.3 Sexual Harassment and Gender-Based Harassment

correspond with the legal definitions. According to a survey (2017) that dealt with data from seven European countries, namely Germany, the UK, France, Sweden, Denmark, Finland and Norway, there appears to be a consensus among the respondents in all of these countries in that if a man touches a woman's bottom or offers her his sexual services, this is sexual harassment (94–97% agree in the first scenario, 86–92% agree in the second one), whereas the scenario in which a man tells a woman a sex joke or looks at her breasts finds more understanding in Germany and Denmark than in the UK, France and Finland.[8] In Germany only 35% of the respondents thought that telling sex jokes was sexual harassment, and in Denmark the percentage was even lower, 17%, in stark contrast to the figures of the UK (69%), France (53%) and Finland (67%). Respectively, only 29% of Germans and 26% of Danes considered looking at a woman's breasts as sexual harassment, compared to 50% of respondents in the UK, 51% in France and in 47% Finland.[9]

In the past few years, sexual harassment in higher education has been the topic of numerous studies, but it is fairly difficult to compare their results, and the differences between countries are remarkable. According to a systematic review of highly cited research papers in scientific journals, the exposure to sexual harassment in higher education "varies between 11 and 73 per cent for heterosexual women (median 49 per cent) and between 3 and 26 per cent for heterosexual men (median 15 per cent)" (Bondestam and Lundqvist 2020, 403). For now, there is little research on sexual harassment or gender harassment in philosophy specifically. For this reason, it is difficult to estimate exactly how common sexual harassment is within philosophy, how philosophy compares with other fields, and what the differences between different countries or departments are. One thing is clear, however: sexual and gender harassment do exist within philosophy, even if they may not be a part of the everyday interaction in the classroom, among students and at the department.

Of course, heterosexual cis women are not the only targets of sexual and gender harassment; heterosexual men and sexual and gender minorities can be targeted, as is becoming increasingly clear thanks to the increased readiness of individuals to speak out about their experiences. Many cases may still remain hidden, however, due to the fact that the targets may experience the incidents too hurtful or shameful to discuss them openly. It is also possible that they do not expect to be believed, or they may consider their case as unique rather than symptomatic of a larger problem. As the targets are often young women who have very little power, they may choose not to risk their career development by speaking out.

---

[8] Yougov.de, Lisa Inhoffen, "Sexuelle Belästigung gegenüber Frauen: Wo fängt sie an und wo hört sie auf?" https://yougov.de/news/2017/11/09/sexuelle-belastigung-gegenuber-frauen-wo-fangt-sie/. Accessed 31 March 2022. In a Danish study, the researchers found differences between women and men in how they related to acts of sexual harassment and what kind of behaviours they interpreted as sexual harassment. They also found a similar characteristic in the Danish attitudes towards sex jokes as did the more international study mentioned above: Danish university students were less likely to interpret them as sexual harassment than non-Danish university students (Guschke et al. 2019).

[9] Ibid.

In interview, Black women philosophers also suggest that the stereotype of Black women as maids or prostitutes affects how they are viewed by other staff members (Allen 2008, 170–172; see also Hill Collins 2009, 142–145 and Dotson 2012). This phenomenon of sexualisation is not limited to Black women philosophers, for it has been demonstrated that women of different minorities are often sexualised (Shimizu 2007). It is as if some applied a different set of rules on how to act towards women in their ingroup and outgroup. Of course, young women can be said to be sexualised also as a group: they are the objects of most of the inappropriate behaviour.

In addition, trans women, trans men and genderqueer individuals face other kinds of challenges in academia. As transgender individuals often have to endure harsh attitudes and rejection by people close to them as well as by strangers, diverse problems may accumulate in their lives, so that they may not make it to academia at all. Once in academia, their gender identity may be misrecognised, or they may be offended on its basis. Sometimes people are pressured to state their "actual" gender. Needless to say, for those who belong to many marginalised groups, that is, for instance, for Black trans women, the situation may be quite fraught despite the seemingly liberal attitudes in academia.[10]

On the basis of the NASEM report, sexual and gender minorities are more likely than other individuals to encounter gender-based harassment, as are those individuals who question gender norms in their behaviour or appearance. More precisely, lesbian or bisexual women, and women who endorse gender-egalitarian beliefs, or who are considered "masculine", encounter gender-based harassment at higher rates than other women. Similarly, transgender, petite or gay men experience more gender-based harassment than other men (NASEM 2018, 27). According another American study, 75.2% of undergraduate students who belonged to the TGQN group (those identifying as transgender, genderqueer, non-conforming, questioning, or as something not listed on the survey), reported being harassed. The percentage of harassed cis female undergraduate students was also alarmingly high, 61.9% (Cantor et al. 2017, xvi).

Having been harassed does not presuppose that this occurs on a daily basis, of course, but even so, harassment should be taken seriously and acted against in and outside the classroom (see e.g. Meyer 2008). In addition to the overt forms of harassment and discrimination there are subtler discriminatory mechanisms, such as implicit bias, stereotype threat and micro-inequities. These are introduced in the following section.

1.4 Subtle Mechanisms of Discrimination: Implicit Bias, Micro-Inequities and Stereotype Threat

Implicit bias, micro-inequity and stereotype threat are originally psychological and sociological concepts that are used to describe those marginalising phenomena that

---

[10] On the difficulty of researching transgender theory in academia, see Grearey 2016.

are difficult to address precisely because of their "invisibility". In philosophy, these issues have been discussed in detail in Katrina Hutchison's and Fiona Jenkins's (eds) (2013) *Women in Philosophy: What Needs to Change?* New York, NY: Oxford University Press.

Implicit bias refers to unconscious biases that affect our ways of perceiving and evaluating people from the targeted groups. Implicit bias affects individuals of all genders, which means that even other women tend to evaluate the achievements of women more negatively than they would if they thought they were evaluating men's achievements. For instance, the same curriculum vitae can be assessed as better and the person behind as deserving of a higher salary, if the name at the top of it is male (Moss-Racusin et al. 2008; Saul 2013, 41). This said, it does not appear to be the case that implicit bias could always be found in assessments (see Birch et al. 2016). Yet the existence of implicit bias in academia has been demonstrated by a number of studies (e.g. Moss-Racusin 2012; Steinpreis 1999), and although these have not targeted philosophers specifically, there is little reason to presume that philosophers would be freer from implicit bias than other academics (see Saul 2013, 43–44).

Another mechanism of subtle discrimination is that of micro-inequities. These are "small harms" such as disrespectful gestures, being ignored or singled out on the basis of characteristics such as sex, race or age. It has been suggested that when they accumulate over time, they can result in low self-esteem and poor career success. The target and the perpetrator may both be unaware of the continuum of micro-inequities that they are involved in and that may slowly undermine the target's chances of a satisfactory career in the extremely competitive field of philosophy. (Brennan 2013, 184–185.) Unsurprisingly, micro-inequities are intimately connected to implicit bias: we are more likely engage in them, if we are implicitly biased against individual members of targeted groups.[11]

According to Samantha Brennan, the flip side of micro-inequities is the genius treatment received by some. She argues that academics may "detect" budding geniuses on rather flimsy grounds, and that the heightened expectations and good career opportunities faced by the chosen ones may in fact produce their good performances. (Brennan 2013, 185.) In a like manner, negative expectations can affect the performance of targeted individuals negatively.

As the phenomenon of stereotype threat shows, this may not even require any belittling attitudes on the part of the members of the dominant group. When individuals of a stigmatised group are preoccupied with fears of confirming the stereotypes about their group, they often do worse in their tasks than they would otherwise. Jennifer Saul argues that stereotype threat can be provoked simply by visual reminders of the group's underrepresentation in the field. In philosophy, situations like this occur easily, for instance, when a woman is presenting her work to an all-male audience in a room decorated with pictures of male philosophers. (Saul 2013, 41–42, 46–47.)

---

[11] For a general discussion on the measures that can be taken to make the atmosphere of a department more welcoming towards women, see Brennan and Corless (2009).

The problem with these subtle mechanisms of discrimination is that they are difficult for all parties to detect. Even if the targets identify these mechanisms at some level, they may be inclined to accuse themselves of paranoia. After all, they are not consistently harassed, and often they can only fathom the different kind of treatment some of their peers receive. The perpetrators, on the other hand, may consider themselves as enlightened people who embrace the ideals of equality and justice. It may be very hard for us to understand our own contribution to a culture of such subtle inequities, especially if we come from a privileged background.

The good news is that there are many ways to loosen the hold of the described inequities, and some of these are easy to put into action. For instance, we can make sure that the web pages and promotional videos of the discipline do not present the students and faculty in a narrow way (i.e. according to the White, male, able-bodied norm). Adding pictures of women philosophers, Black philosophers and Asian philosophers on the wall, to complement the row of White male philosophers, is a gesture that does not tax the department budget too heavily.

Even so, the example at hand brings us to the core of the resistance of philosophy towards change. We may be generous and fair in principle, but when we are asked to redefine philosophy to include "the others", we tend to become less generous. This generosity does not necessarily exist even between Western philosophers of different philosophical leanings: what the other is doing, is not philosophy at all, or at best a caricature of philosophy.

Philosophy is precious to us philosophers, something we want to protect and cherish. At the same time, we tend to live within a very specific form of it, becoming habituated with its modes of thought and preferred questions, and the cultural heritage it carries. It is precisely this form of philosophical life that we wish to protect. For this reason, while we may be ready to increase diversity in the student body and staff, this readiness depends on the form of philosophical life that the persons in question have adopted as theirs. This policy shuts out those who might challenge the dominant views about philosophy, its limits and most central questions.

Consequently, making philosophy more inclusive may imply negotiations about the nature of philosophy. Kristie Dotson has argued that this transformation presupposes the following changes: (a) increasing the visibility and impact of underrepresented groups by hiring more people from these groups as staff, and (b) increasing diversity in the curriculum, so that questions that are of particular interest to the philosophers and students of the underrepresented groups are covered (Dotson 2012, 17). The problem is that even if steps towards this direction are taken, the work of the new hires may remain isolated from the general development of the discipline.[12] Positive discrimination can also raise doubts about the competence of scholars belonging to the underrepresented groups.[13]

---

[12] Dotson discussed this idea in her keynote lecture "On the Value of Challenging Philosophical Orthodoxy: A Tale of Two Careers", in the conference *Feminist Utopias: Transforming the Present of Philosophy*, in Reykjavík, 30 March 2017.

[13] There are numerous reports by American women philosophers at the site *What Is It Like to Be a Woman in Philosophy?* on complaints about how they got their position "only because they are women".

Change may be quite slow or non-existent when there are no real incentives for hiring individuals from underrepresented groups in academia. In Finland, the Equality Act of 1986 makes it possible for organisations to voluntarily use positive discrimination. This does not appear to produce results: it does not raise the percentage of women in the hired staff. (Husu 2007, 98.) The situation might be improved by endorsing a diversity of philosophical traditions in the curriculum and staff appointments, but, at least at the surface level, this goal appears to be in contradiction with the politics of education that demands departments to create recognisable profiles, in other words, to focus on specific themes and approaches. Acknowledging the situation, however, can help develop profiles that acquire depth through specific subthemes, for instance by intersecting with disability, feminist or Black studies. In other words, the problem does not have to remain unresolved: it is possible to combine specialisation and inclusiveness.

1.5 The Structure of the Book

By now, I have provided an overall discussion of the theme of women's underrepresentation in philosophy, especially among philosophy students, summarising a number of empirical studies on the question. Chapter 2 discusses the role of pedagogical choices and philosophical conceptualisations in questioning and undoing power hierarchies. More precisely, I introduce some of the approaches and goals within feminist pedagogy in general and in the Gender and Philosophy summer schools, which will be discussed in more detail in the following chapters. In addition, I elucidate the concepts of "situation" and "alienation", which provide the framework for the rest of the book.

Chapter 3, "The Historical Situation", is the first of three chapters that describe and analyse the different aspects of the philosophy student's situation. In this chapter I demonstrate how subjects—in this case philosophy students—should always be understood as subjects in time, who project themselves towards the future while being rooted in a specific historical soil. After a phenomenological discussion of temporality, I describe and criticise Michèle Le Dœuff's psychoanalytically informed idea of the erotico-theoretical transference of women in philosophy. I also investigate the student's relationship to the philosophical canon, analysing the possibilities of intimacy in the reading experience as well as those of idolatry, or the cult of the genius. I demonstrate why bringing forward the work and ideas of women predecessors is important, and propose a transformation in how the history of philosophy is considered: the historical ground should not consist of only the White and male canon, through which the history of philosophy is usually narrated, but also of the less-known voices of women and people of colour, through which another kind of historical "we" could be formed. Through a discussion of an experimental summer school titled Feminist Thought in Historical Perspective, I illustrate how the voices of women philosophers can be integrated into the discussion of the history of philosophy.

While the background survey and interviews inform all of the book, the student perspectives provided by them are elucidated particularly in Chap. 4, "The Affective, Social and Bodily Situation". The chapter starts with a discussion of the emotional situation of students especially on women students' passion for and alienation from philosophy. I then analyse the significance of students' class and ethnic background for studying philosophy, demonstrating that, apart from the gender-related alienation, many other kinds of alienations can manifest themselves in the insecurities of philosophy students. In addition, I examine the tendency of philosophy teaching to distance itself from all the factual differences in embodied existence in favour of universalisation, and consider the possibility to teach from the viewpoint of the senses, engaging the body as a unity of the senses. I also demonstrate how the questions of the "disembodiment" of philosophy and of the tendency to shut feelings outside philosophical discussions were tackled in the summer school titled Philosophy of the Body by means of focusing practices, thinking "from the body". In contrast, the summer school titled Feminist Political Philosophy included feminist analyses of violence, perspectives of the Global South and intersectionality, psychoanalytic theories, and discussions of universalism and difference, using problem-based learning as its pedagogical point of departure.

Chapter 5, "The Moral Situation", explores the possibilities of feminist ethics in teaching philosophy and the ways in which it can deal with power struggles in the classroom. In this connection, I discuss the concept of generosity as it is conveyed in Beauvoir's philosophy and in Debra Bergoffens's analysis of it (1997). These philosophers describe generosity as an attitude towards the other that accepts the other's freedom and allows the other to freely take or leave the gift that is offered to them. Furthermore, I demonstrate that care and generosity could and very often do act as ethical points of departure in teaching philosophy, and that cultivating these helps pass them on to new generations of philosophers. The chapter ends with a discussion of an experimental course on Care Ethics and Conflicts, in which students were invited to examine and discuss how experience, reason and emotion played a part in our moral reasoning.

The concluding chapter summarises the insights of the earlier chapters and suggests some possible questions for empirical research on the underrepresentation of women and other minorities in philosophy. In addition, I provide a checklist about the minimal requirements for teaching philosophy inclusively. This makes it easy even for the hastiest reader to think through better practices of teaching philosophy. Chapter 6 ends with a discussion of the political reality in which philosophy is taught, evaluating the possibilities for resistance in the context of diminishing resources and asking how we can act against the currents of politics of austerity, extreme competitiveness and precarisation of academic work. In addition, I discuss the possibilities of philosophy in crisis situations, and the philosophy class as a stronghold of intellectual freedom.

During the time I have worked on the manuscript of this book, we have experienced two globally significant events with pedagogical consequences. The first is the second rise of the #MeToo movement since 2017. The questions raised by the movement led me to discuss sexual and gender harassment in more detail in the introduction than had initially been my intention. The second globally significant event is the COVID-19 pandemic since 2020. Due to the pandemic, universities moved most of their teaching online. In terms of pedagogical possibilities and choices, the change is enormous and one that is likely to continue to have an effect on post-pandemic education. Remote learning benefits some students but appears to be detrimental to the majority in a situation in which informal face-to-face interaction is scarce. Whether or not this development has gendered effects, remains to be seen. While I was unable to provide an in-depth discussion in the context of this publication, I would venture to suggest that for the most part, the discussion of gender, situatedness and alienation can be adapted to different learning platforms without too many complications. Other ongoing crises, such as climate change and wars, are not discussed at length, even though I do acknowledge that they challenge the future-orientation of young people in particular and thereby have a significant effect on learning situations.

Finally, I want to address the criticism that my emphasis on the genders "woman" and "man" may generate. To focus on women does not mean that I would deny the reality of the gender spectrum, which includes genders such as "genderfluid", "agender" and "uncertain". Nor do I challenge the fact that in some instances a genderfluid or nonbinary person, for instance, can be misinterpreted as a woman, which can occasionally make it problematic to make generalisations about the genders of groups of people. For practical reasons, however, I have had to restrict the focus of my study to the underrepresented group that is most visible in philosophy and in the empirical studies I discuss in the book, namely people who identify themselves as women. In this definition, I include both cis and trans women. This said, I acknowledge that the experiences of cis women and trans women can differ in significant ways. The specific experience of the latter is discussed in Chap. 4.[14]

One central issue in the book is the relationship between power and freedom. Often philosophical education is considered as intrinsically liberating—but is it? When and why does it create hierarchies and alienation? Are power hierarchies unavoidable in education? In what follows I highlight the ways in which feminist pedagogy has tackled the issues of power hierarchies and diversity.

---

[14] The category of cisgender refers to those who identify with the gender defined for them in birth, and usually also express themselves according to that gender. The term cis woman (or cis female), then, would refer to those who identify themselves with the gender "woman" defined for them in birth, and usually express themselves according to this gender. (About the formation and use of the term, see e.g. Enke 2012.) These definitions have sometimes been seen as problematic, because individuals may experience different levels of estrangement from the social category of women depending on the situation, even if they do not challenge their categorisation as women as such. Yet I believe that although these terms do not account for all the nuances of the lived reality of gender identities, they will go through a similar normalisation over time as the term "heterosexual". The latter term acquired its current meaning only in 1934, when Karl Maria Kertbeny paired it off with the term "homosexual" in order to refer to those, who are attracted to individuals of the "opposite" sex (e.g. Herzer 1985). The introduction and acceptance of the term of the term "cisgender" brings about a change of paradigm in how we interpret gender identity: no longer in terms of normality and deviance but in terms of diversity.

References

Alcoff, Linda (ed.). 2003. *Singing in the Fire: Stories of Women in Philosophy*. Lanham: Rowman and Littlefield Publishers.
Allen, Anita. 2008. Situated Voices: Black Women in/on the Profession of Philosophy. *Hypatia* 23 (2): 160–189.
Antony, Louise. 2012. Different Voices or Perfect Storm: Why Are There So Few Women in Philosophy? *Journal of Social Philosophy* 43 (3): 227–255.
Aristotle. 2001. *Poetics: 350 BC*. Trans. Samuel Henry Butcher. South Bend, IN: Blacksburg, VA: Infomotions, Inc.; Virginia Tech.
Beebee, Helen and Jenny Saul. 2011. *Women in Philosophy in the UK: A Report by the British Philosophical Association and the Society for Women in Philosophy UK*. A Report by the British Philosophical Association and the Society for Women in Philosophy UK. https://bpa.ac.uk/wp-content/uploads/2018/11/BPA_Report_Women_In_Philosophy.pdf. Accessed 29 April 2022.
Beebee, Helen and Jenny Saul. 2021. *Women in Philosophy in the UK*. On behalf of the British Philosophical Association and the Society for Women in Philosophy UK. https://bpa.ac.uk/wp-content/uploads/2021/11/2021-BPA-SWIP-Report-Women-in-Philosophy-in-the-UK.pdf. Accessed 29 April 2022.
Bergoffen, Debra B. 1997. *The Philosophy of Simone De Beauvoir: Gendered Phenomenologies, Erotic Generosities*. Albany, NY: State University of New York Press.
Birch, Phil, John Batten, and Jo Batey. 2016. The Influence of Student Gender on the Assessment of Undergraduate Student Work. *Assessment & Evaluation in Higher Education* 41 (7): 1065–1080.
Bishop, Glenys, with Helen Beebee, Eliza Goddard and Ardiane Rini. 2013. Seeing Trends in the Data. 2013. In *Women in Philosophy: What Needs to Change?* eds Katrina Hutchison and Fiona Jenkins, 231–252. New York, NY: Oxford University Press.
Bondestam, Fredrik and Maja Lundqvist. 2020. Sexual Harassment in Higher education: A Systematic Review. *European Journal of Higher Education*. https://www.tandfonline.com/doi/pdf/https://doi.org/10.1080/21568235.2020.1729833?needAccess=true. Accessed 3 April 2020.
Brennan, Samantha. 2013. Rethinking the Moral Significance of Micro-Inequities: The Case of Women in Philosophy. In *Women in Philosophy: What Needs to Change?* eds Katrina Hutchison and Fiona Jenkins, 180–196. New York, NY: Oxford University Press.
Brennan, Samantha and Rob Corless. 2009. Creating a Warmer Environment for Women in the Mathematical Sciences and in Philosophy. *Western Arts and Humanities* 33 (2): 54–61.
Brownstein, Michael and Jennifer Saul (eds). 2016a. *Implicit Bias and Philosophy: Metaphysics and Epistemology*. Oxford, UK: Oxford University Press.
Brownstein, Michael and Jennifer Saul (eds). 2016b. *Implicit Bias and Philosophy: Moral Responsibility, Structural Injustice, and Ethics*. Oxford, UK: Oxford University Press.
Cantor, David, Bonnie Fisher, Susan Chibnall, Reanne Townsend, Hyunshik Lee, Carol Bruce and Gail Thomas. 2017. *Report on the AAU Campus Climate Survey on Sexual Assault and Sexual Misconduct*. Rockville, MD: Westatt.
Cooper, Bridget. 2011. *Empathy in Education: Engagement, Values and Achievement*. London: Continuum.
Demarest, Heather, Seth Robertson, Megan Haggard, Madeline Martin-Seaver and Jewelle Bickel. 2017. Similarity and Enjoyment: Predicting Continuation for Women in Philosophy. *Analysis* 77 (3): 525–541.
Dotson, Kristie. 2012. How is this Paper Philosophy? *Comparative Philosophy* 3 (1): 3–29. http://scholarworks.sjsu.edu/cgi/viewcontent.cgi?article=1039&context=comparativephilosophy. Accessed 22 April 2022.
Dougherty, Tom, Samuel Baron and Kristie Miller. 2015. Why do Female Students Leave Philosophy? The Story from Sydney. *Hypatia* 30 (2): 467–474.
Enke, Finn A. 2012. The Education of Little Cis: Cisgender and the Discipline of Opposing Bodies. In *Transfeminist Perspectives in and Beyond Gender and Gender Studies*, ed. Anne Enke, 60–77. Philadelphia, PA: Temple University Press.

References

Finnish Act on Equality between Women and Men, Equality Act, 27. https://julkaisut.valtio neuvosto.fi/bitstream/handle/10024/75131/Act_on%20Equality_between_women_and_men_ 2015_FINAL.pdf?sequence=1. Accessed 31 March 2022.

Friedman, Marilyn. 2013. Women in Philosophy: Why Should We Care? In *Women in Philosophy : What Needs to Change?* eds Katrina Hutchison and Fiona Jenkins, 21–38. New York, NY: Oxford University Press.

Grearey, Markisha. 2016. A Proposal for Doing Transgender Theory. In *Reclaiming Genders: Transsexual Grammars at the Fin De Siecle*, eds Kate More and Stephen Whittle, 159–170. London: Bloomsbury.

Guschke, Bontu Lucie, Kaitlin Busse, Farhiya Khalid, Sara Louise Muhr and Sine Nørholm Just. 2019. Sexual Harassment in Higher Education - Experiences and Perceptions among Students at a Danish University. *Kvinder, Køn & Forskning*, 28 (1–2): 11–30

Heinämaa, Sara. 2000. *Ihmetys ja rakkaus: esseitä ruumiin ja sukupuolen fenomenologiasta*. Helsinki: Nemo.

Heinämaa, Sara. 2017. Love and Admiration (Wonder): Fundaments of the Self-Other Relations. In *Emotional Experiences: Ethical and Social Significance*, eds John J. Drummond and Sonja Rinofner-Kreidl, 155–174. London: Policy Network.

Hill Collins, Patricia. 2009. *Black Feminist Thought: Knowledge, Consciousness, and the Politics of Empowerment*. New York, NY: Routledge.

Husu, Liisa. 2007. Women in Universities in Finland: Relative Advances and Continuing Contradictions. In *Women, Universities and Change*, ed. Mary Ann Dagowitz Sagaria. New York: Palgrave MacMillan, 89–111.

Hutchison, Katrina and Fiona Jenkins (eds). 2013. *Women in Philosophy: What Needs to Change?* New York, NY: Oxford University Press.

Herzer, M. 1985. Kertbeny and the Nameless Love. *Journal of Homosexuality* 12 (1): 1. http://www.ncbi.nlm.nih.gov/pubmed/3913702. Accessed 22 April 2022.

Illeris, Knud. 2014. *Transformative Learning and Identity*. Abingdon, Oxon: Routledge.

Inhoffen, Lisa. 2017. Sexuelle Belästigung gegenüber Frauen: Wo fängt sie an und wo hört sie auf? Yougov.de, https://yougov.de/news/2017/11/09/sexuelle-belastigung-gegenuber-frauen-wo-fangt-sie/. Accessed 29 April 2022.

Irigaray, Luce. 1989. *Éthique de la différence sexuelle*. Collection Critique. Paris: Minuit.

Jenkins, Fiona. 2013. Singing the Post-Discrimination Blues: Notes for a Critique of Academic Meritocracy. In *Women in Philosophy: What Needs to Change*, eds Hutchison Katrina and Fiona Jenkins, 81–102. New York, NY: Oxford University Press.

Leuschner, Anne. 2019. Why So Low? On Indirect Effects of Gender Bias in Philosophy. *Metaphilosophy* 50 (3), 231–249.

Ma, Debbie, Clennie Webster, Nanae Tachibe, and Robert Gressis. 2017. 21% Versus 79%: Explaining Philosophy's Gender Disparities with Stereotyping and Identification. *Philosophical Psychology*: 1–21. http://www.tandfonline.com/doi/pdf/https://doi.org/10.1080/09515089.2017. 1363881n?needAccess=true. Accessed 22 April 2022

Meyer, Elizabeth J. 2008. A Feminist Reframing of Bullying and Harassment: Transforming Schools through Critical Pedagogy. *McGill Jounal of Education / Revue des sciences de l'éducation de McGill*, 43 (1), May 2008. https://mje.mcgill.ca/article/view/1077. Accessed 12 October 2022.

Moss-Racusin, Corinne A. 2012. Science Faculty's Subtle Gender Biases Favor Male Students. *Proceedings of the National Academy of Sciences of the United States of America* 109 (41): 16474–16479.

NASEM. 2018. *Sexual Harassment of Women: Climate, Culture, and Consequences in Academic Sciences, Engineering, and Medicine,* Consensus Study Report of The National Academies of Sciences, Engineering and Medicine, eds Paula A. Johnson, Sheila E. Widnall and Franzier F. Beneya; Committee on the Impacts of Sexual harassment in Academia, Committee on Women in Science, Engineering, and Medicine Policy and Global Affairs. Washington DC: The National Academies Press.

Paxton, Molly, Carrie Figdor and Valerie Tiberius. 2012. Quantifying the Gender Gap: An Empirical Study of the Underrepresentation of Women in Philosophy. *Hypatia* 27 (4) 949–957.

Reuter, Martina. 2015. Varför så få kvinnor? Könsfördelningen inom den akademiska filosofin. *Tidskrift för politisk filosofi* 19 (3): 5–19. http://www.politiskfilosofi.se/fulltext/2015-3/TPF_2015-3_05-19_reuter.html. Accessed 22 April 2022.

Saul, Jennifer. 2013. Implicit Bias, Stereotype Threat, and Women in Philosophy. In *Women in Philosophy: What Needs to Change?* eds Katrina Hutchison and Fiona Jenkins, 39–60. New York, NY: Oxford University Press.

Shimizu, Celine Parreñas. 2007. *The Hypersexuality of Race: Performing Asian American Women on Screen and Scene*. Durham, NC: Duke University Press.

Simons, Margaret A. and Erika Ruonakoski. 2021. Margaret A. Simons, Rebel at Heart: Civil Rights Activist, Feminist, Beauvoir Scholar. *Simone de Beauvoir Studies*, 31 (2), 317–335.

Statistics Finland, the, the Ministry of Culture and Education and the Finnish National Agency for Education. Vipunen: Education Statistics Finland. https://vipunen.fi/en-gb/university/Pages/Hakeneet-ja-hyväksytyt.aspx. Accessed 19 April 2022.

Steinpreis, Rhea. 1999. The Impact of Gender on the Review of the Curricula Vitae of Job Applicants and Tenure Candidates: A National Empirical Study. *Sex Roles* 41 (7): 509–528.

Sveinsdóttir, Ásta. 2011. Metaphysics of Sex and Gender. In *Feminist Metaphysics*, ed. Charlotte Witt, 47–65. Dordrecht: Springer.

Thompson Morgan, Toni Adleberg, Sam Sims and Eddy Nahmias. 2016. Why Do Women Leave Philosophy? Surveying Students at the Introductory Level. *Philosopher's Imprint* 16 (6), 1–36. http://quod.lib.umich.edu/p/phimp/3521354.0016.006/1. Accessed 28 Jan 2018.

Thorgeirsdottir Sigridur. 2020. The Torn Robe of Philosophy: Philosophy as a Woman in *The Consolation of Philosophy* by Boethius. In *Methodological Reflections on Women's Contribution and Influence in the History of Philosophy*, eds Sigridur Thorgeirsdottir and Ruth Edith Hagengruber, 83–95. Cham: Springer.

Witt, Charlotte. 2011. *The Metaphysics of Gender*. Oxford: Oxford University Press.

What Is It Like to Be a Woman in Philosophy? https://beingawomaninphilosophy.wordpress.com. Accessed 31 March 2022.

What We're Doing About What It's Like, which deals with the institutional and individual responses to problems for women in philosophy. https://whatweredoingaboutwhatitslike.wordpress.com. Accessed 31 March 2022.

White, Richard. 2016. Nietzsche on Generosity and the Gift-Giving Virtue. *British Journal for the History of Philosophy* 24 (2): 348–364.

Young, Michael. 1963. *The Rise of the Meritocracy 1870–2033: An Essay on Education and Equality*. Harmondsworth: Penguin Books.

Open Access This chapter is licensed under the terms of the Creative Commons Attribution 4.0 International License (http://creativecommons.org/licenses/by/4.0/), which permits use, sharing, adaptation, distribution and reproduction in any medium or format, as long as you give appropriate credit to the original author(s) and the source, provide a link to the Creative Commons license and indicate if changes were made.

The images or other third party material in this chapter are included in the chapter's Creative Commons license, unless indicated otherwise in a credit line to the material. If material is not included in the chapter's Creative Commons license and your intended use is not permitted by statutory regulation or exceeds the permitted use, you will need to obtain permission directly from the copyright holder.

Chapter 2
Undoing Power Hierarchies

Abstract What alternatives have been created within feminist pedagogy to question power hierarchies and to make teaching more inclusive? What approaches were adopted in the Gender and Philosophy summer schools in order to achieve these goals? After discussing these questions, I demonstrate how the concepts of "alienation" and "situation" can be used to analyse power dynamics and the framework they provide to the rest of the book.

2.1 Feminist Pedagogy

The idea of education as a powerful tool for change is not new. Plato suggested the idea that the right kind of education allows both women and men make full use of their talents and help create the ideal state. Later many women thinkers from Christine de Pizan (1405/1999) to Catharine Macaulay (1790/2014) voiced the idea that it is impossible learn about the real intellectual potential of women without providing them an education that is as good as that of men. Also Mary Wollstonecraft (1792/2000) argued that giving women a rational education will allow them to contribute to the activities of the society in a more comprehensive manner.

When thinking through the question of inclusion in the teaching of philosophy, one of the most obvious reference points are those of feminist pedagogy. For feminist pedagogy, the idea of change through education—the ideals of liberation and empowerment—has been essential. This is no wonder considering that the roots of feminist pedagogy are in the feminist movement and in feminist theorisation. Another important source for feminist pedagogy has been critical pedagogy, which has critical theory as its starting point and is described as a pedagogy of liberation. Here Paulo Freire's thinking and especially his *Pedagogy of the Oppressed* (1970/1972) have been influential. The work of bell hooks, such as her famous *Teaching to Transgress* (1994), is influenced by Freire. Freire advocates dialogical learning, which is meant to enable members of the oppressed groups to get their voices heard. They share their experiences, become aware of their possibilities as political agents, and finally, act for their own liberation. These ideas are shared by many feminist theorists. In fact the feminist practice of consciousness raising, which became widely known in the late 1960s, has been compared to and sometimes equated with Freire's conscientisation (*conscienzaçao*) or critical consciousness. At the same time, his lack of concern for gender issues has been criticised (see e.g. Luke and Gore (eds) 1992).

All in all, the different trends in feminist pedagogy have followed the shifts in feminist theory. Consciousness raising was primarily a technique of radical feminism, according to which the society was, inherently, a patriarchy and women its oppressed class. Consciousness raising groups were a way of learning about what it is to be a woman, and how personal and private experiences were related to the social reality. The sharing of experiences was a basis for political action. In a way, the later Internet-based feminist movements such as #MeToo can be seen as followers of consciousness raising groups, with the difference that now the personal experience is not shared only among peers but made public.

Another technique of feminist pedagogy that shares some features with consciousness raising is memory work. While consciousness raising had its roots in the New York of the 1960s, memory work is a method invented by a German sociologist and philosopher, Frigga Haug, in the 1980s. Memory work, which is likewise practised in a group, involves writing about specific memories followed by reciprocal commenting on them. The idea is to question the boundary between subject and object of research: the group is a group of co-researchers. The task is to learn about social structures through the memories of individual women (Haug et al. 1987; Onyx and Small 2001).

The concerns of feminism have broadened to cover the issues of different marginalised groups, including sexual, gender and ethnic minorities, as well as women of colour. The introduction of the term "intersectionality"[1] in the late 1980s by Kimberlé Crenshaw was particularly important to the development of feminist pedagogy, for it facilitated the understanding that the marginalisations of different groups can affect each other, and, in particular, how one person may be marginalised in a number of ways (see also Hill Collins 2009, 15, 138–145). This implies that in a classroom, lecturers should develop their sensitivities towards minority students and find practices that allow an atmosphere of trust to develop and different viewpoints to become expressed (e.g. Caporale-Bizzini and Richter Malabotta (eds) 2009). The theory of intersectionality has gradually gained a more and more prominent position in feminist pedagogy, and, despite some criticisms, it remains central. In this book, questions related to intersecting marginalisations are discussed primarily in Chap. 4.

Initiatives have been taken to engage meditative and body awareness practices such as mindfulness in learning, and attention has been paid also to how space and the way it is used contribute to the learning situation and issues of hierarchy in the classroom (e.g. Asher 2003; Thompson 2017; Schalk et al. 2017). One of the most recent influences comes from posthumanism, which has led theorists of education to

---

[1] The term "intersectionality" was coined already in 1989, but it was only with third-wave feminism that it achieved its status. Kathryn T. Gines has traced the earliest expressions of proto-theories of intersectionality to the 1830s, in, for instance, Maria Stewart's pamphlet (1831) and Anna Julia Cooper's collection of speeches (1892), in which she discusses the particular position of Black women as outsiders to the debates on both gender and race (Gines 2011, 276).

consider the relevance of non-human agents for learning processes (e.g. Radomska 2013; see also Jokinen and Rautio 2016). Both body awareness practices and the relationship to non-human nature in learning philosophy are discussed in Chap. 4, in the context of the summer school held in Reykjavík.

To be sure, feminist pedagogy has not developed separately from other pedagogical trends. In fact, quite a few of its methods are used outside feminist pedagogy, which is understandable in the light of the current popularity of the student-centred approach. For instance, memory work is also used in social pedagogy.

Another issue that has become topical in the context of feminist pedagogy is trigger or content warnings, which were originally used by bloggers to flag content about sexual violence. The aim is not to warn everybody about all potentially challenging content but to take traumatised audience members into account. For them, presumably, facing such a topic might cause physical symptoms, in which case it could be helpful for them to prepare themselves, or to have the choice to leave the room before the situation gets too difficult to bear. It has been suggested that content warnings function as a code, signalling that traumatised individuals are taken into account.

It remains unclear, however, what the right policy would be from the point of view of students. Some researchers argue against the beneficial effect of trigger warnings on students (e.g. Sanson et al., 2019).[2] For now, many lecturers use trigger warnings by choice, and in the United States many universities demand that their faculty use trigger warnings so as to avoid lawsuits. In philosophy, a wide variety of subfields are unlikely to deal with emotionally distressful content, but others handle topics such as torture and sexual violence that require the lecturer to adopt a policy regarding trigger warnings. It is good to keep in mind that there are other ways to create a safe and open atmosphere in the classroom, such as a discussion of ethical concerns in the beginning of a course.

How does inclusive teaching of philosophy then relate to the broader context of feminist pedagogy? Surely there is no one correct way of teaching philosophy any more than there is one correct way of teaching anything else, for the "right" methods of teaching tend to depend at least partly on the personalities of individual lecturers. This said, it is clear that feminist pedagogy can at the very least sensitise the teaching staff to the question of the other: how do I as a lecturer relate to the other that is different from myself in terms of gender identity, race, ethnicity, religion, sexual orientation, social class, able-bodiedness, and so on? Is it my task to teach the students to conform to a tacit norm or to provide possibilities for the diversity of students to learn as themselves? This is a theme particularly prominent in bell hooks's *Teaching to Transgress*. One of hooks's concerns is how Black students have to adapt to the White norm in mixed schools, whereas in Black schools they are allowed a history of their own, a learning environment that supports them in their

---

[2] Megan Sanson et al. (2019) are concerned that the widespread adoption of trigger warnings may further increase anxiousness in students. It is argued that if trigger warnings encourage avoidance behaviour in people with symptoms of PTSD, they are actually harmful in the long run. Benjamin W. Bellet et al. (2018) likewise suggest that trigger warnings increase anxiety towards allegedly harmful written material and that they reinforce the idea of trauma survivors as vulnerable.

particular situatedness. Without advocating gender separatism in philosophy, I will be discussing the needed strategies to allow women and other minorities find their roots and understand their specific situation within philosophy, rather than giving into feelings of alienation and rootlessness.

Another thing that feminist pedagogy draws attention to are the power struggles, power structures and hierarchies in the classroom. As I demonstrate in Chap. 5, these struggles are constantly present and observable. To be sure, many of the methods and exercises of feminist pedagogy can be imaginatively applied to the teaching of philosophy. Yet it is good to acknowledge that in disciplines that focus on power relations, such as gender studies, or education itself, it may be easier than in philosophy to motivate the spending of a considerable amount of time on reflection of the learning process, or exercises such as the privilege walk,[3] or listening, dancing, improvisation, voice and sound work. In Chap. 4, however, I discuss ways to integrate such exercises in the philosophy class, suggesting that they can be applied fruitfully when the topic of the course supports their use.

Even if the demands of philosophical discourse can at times appear intimidating, for many students the philosophy class is also a kind of safe space, in which to concentrate on intellectual work and thinking together. Conversely, exercises that aim to empower students by engaging their emotions or call for sharing sometimes painful experiences have their own challenges. For this reason, if an experimental approach is taken, it is a good idea to inform the students before the course starts, and to specify the methods clearly in the course description and introduction. This gives the students time to prepare themselves, or to opt out. It is even better if, during the course, students can from time to time choose what type of approach is taken in the class. Even here, however, it should be acknowledged that a group decision can have alienating elements within it: now the dissenting individual feels alienated from the rest of the group rather than from the educational setting dictated from above. In other words, even if feminist and critical pedagogies offer a lot of tools for undoing power hierarchies and for involving the whole body-subject, they cannot entirely eliminate the feelings of not-belonging.

---

[3] In the beginning of the privilege walk the participants stand in a row, and then, depending on their experiences and following the facilitator's instructions, take steps forward or backward. For instance: "If you are white, take a step forward." The idea is to concretise the way privileges work in life, giving you a head start in comparison to the less privileged. The problem is, of course, that the participants can find themselves in a vulnerable position, sharing a lot of information about themselves with people they may not know very well. For an explanation and critique of the privilege walk, see Meg Bolger's "Why I Don't Facilitate Privilege Walks Anymore and What I Do Instead" (2018). https://medium.com/@MegB/why-i-dont-won-t-facilitate-privilege-walks-anymore-and-what-i-do-instead-380c95490e10at. Accessed 4 April 2022.

2.2 Gender and Philosophy Summer Schools

The Gender and Philosophy project organised four experimental summer schools on feminist philosophy.[4] The summer schools were held in four Nordic countries—Iceland, Finland, Denmark and Norway—in the summers of 2016 and 2017. The idea was to experiment with inclusive pedagogies that would be particularly suitable for teaching philosophy. Students were recruited especially in the involved four universities: University of Iceland, University of Jyväskylä, Aalborg University and University of Oslo. Yet some students came from other universities and countries, mainly from Europe and North America, finding information about applying to the summer schools through the diverse networks of the organisers.

The summer schools were all rather different, starting from the number of participating students: the summer schools in Reykjavík, Jyväskylä, Oslo and Aalborg had respectively thirty, forty-one, twenty and twenty-four participants. All four summer schools had a clear female majority: women made up 79% of all the students. The students were expected to have a good background in philosophy. Most of them were master's students, but doctoral students were included. Some of the students attended several of the summer schools.

The order the summer schools are presented in this volume corresponds with the order they were organised in, with the exception of the Icelandic summer school, which was the first one we organised but is presented here second. All in all, the summer schools took quite different pedagogical approaches. The Reykjavík Summer School experimented with body awareness practices, whereas the Finnish summer school integrated the history of feminist thought into the discussion of the history of philosophy. The Danish summer school aimed to provide the students with a clear method, project-oriented—problem-based learning (PO-PBL), as the framework that allows them to work independently and to create their own research questions. The Oslo Summer School addressed the question of inclusion from the perspective of care ethics, taking the different learning styles of students into account by making a variety of learning methods available.

In other words, the summer schools explored the learning and teaching of philosophy each in their own way, pedagogically addressing the questions central to feminist philosophy such as the mind–body split, power hierarchies, the absence of women in the philosophical canon, and the dichotomy between reason and emotions. The summer schools are discussed in more detail at the end of the next three chapters. Before we consider the different aspects of students' situation in these chapters, however, and to better understand the question of inclusion and exclusion, it is necessary to examine the very concepts of "situation" and "alienation" as they are discussed in the history of philosophy.

---

[4] The website of the project can be found here: https://genderandphilosophy.weebly.com. Accessed 4 April 2022.

2.3 Concepts of "Situation" and "Alienation"

In *Being and Nothingness* (1943), Jean-Paul Sartre discusses the concept of situation at length, arguing that freedom only exists in a factual situation that includes one's past, one's spatial place, environment and mortality (2003, 503–573). Beauvoir elaborates on the concept of situation to describe the embodied existence of girls and women in *The Second Sex* (Beauvoir 2008; 2010; see also Beauvoir 1960, 562–563; 1984, 548–549; and Kruks 1998, 51; Ruonakoski 2015, 47–48; 2017, 336–342). According to her, it is within a social, cultural, historical, economical, psychological and bodily situation that a child grows into a woman, a man or a person whose identity does not easily fit into these categories, and embraces or rejects "feminine" or "masculine" attributes and modes of behaviour (Beauvoir 2008; 2010).

For many feminist readers the idea of situatedness may first bring to mind stand-point theory, represented by Nancy Hartsock's and Sandra Harding's work. In stand-point theory situatedness is understood first and foremost as epistemological: marginalised groups are thought to be socially situated in such a manner that they have a more realistic view of the power dynamics than others. In the phenomenological–existentialist tradition, situation is understood in reference to the totality of existence; yet it would be artificial to separate these two views of situation sharply from each other. Both Beauvoir's and Hartsock's philosophies are influenced by G. W. F. Hegel's philosophy and include ideas that bear a resemblance to W. E. B. Du Bois's concept of double consciousness. The concept refers to the consciousness of oppressed subjects—in Du Bois's case Black people—who must be able to observe themselves not only from their own perspective but also from the perspective of their oppressors (see e.g. Du Bois 1964).[5] Hartsock refers to this idea in her discussion of the epistemically privileged vantage point of women in patriarchy (Hartsock 1998, 27, 243).

According to Margaret Simons, Du Bois's racial theory and his concept of double consciousness influenced Beauvoir indirectly through the work of Richard Wright (Simons 1999, 176).[6] This parallel would be visible in her analysis of woman as the secondary and inessential subject, who can become an accomplice in her own subjection, when she accepts man's perspective to her as the primary one (Simons 1999, 176–178). All in all, double consciousness can be seen as a form of alienation, for it presupposes an unwanted distance to oneself, which is mediated through the other's gaze.

---

[5] Du Bois writes: "After the Egyptian and Indian, the Greek and Roman, the Teuton and Mongolian, the Negro is a sort of seventh son, born with a veil, and gifted with second-sight in this American world,—a world which yields him no true self-consciousness, but only lets him see himself through the revelation of the other world. It is a peculiar sensation, this double-consciousness, this sense of always looking at one's self through the eyes of others, of measuring one's soul by the tape of a world that looks on in amused contempt and pity. One ever feels his twoness,—an American, a Negro; two souls, two thoughts, two unreconciled strivings; two warring ideals in one dark body, whose dogged strength alone keeps it from being torn asunder." (Du Bois 1964, 16–17.).

[6] For the connection between Sartre, Beauvoir and Wright, see also Gines 2010.

2.3 Concepts of "Situation" and "Alienation"

Yet my use of the concept of alienation is informed by a wider array of philosophical perspectives. The term is, of course, quite loaded, due to the fact that it has been used in numerous ways in the histories of philosophy, sociology and psychology. One of the divisive issues has been whether alienation should be viewed as a universal human condition or as a historically, socially and psychologically defined state. Even in the works of Hegel, whose discussion on alienation (*Entfremdung, Entäusserung*) had an impact on later generations of philosophers, one can allegedly find two conceptions of the generalisability of the concept. In his earlier writings, Hegel relates alienation to a specific historical moment (his own time and its practice of Christianity),[7] but later he reformulated his theory suggesting that alienation was an integral part of human existence and happens through work. In other words, in their work human beings create objects that express human life, but as human beings themselves change in the process of work, at some point the objects of their work no longer coincide with their purposes, and they cease to recognise the object world as brought into existence by themselves. Karl Marx, instead, argued that alienation is created by the capitalist production system, in which workers cannot identify with the product of their work. (See e.g. Gouldner 1980, 177–181; Lukács 1975, 19; Taylor 1980, 23–41.) Later thinkers, such as Sartre, Jacques Lacan and Jacques Derrida, embraced the idea of alienation as a permanent state of human existence: the self is split, unable to reach the wholeness which it nonetheless seeks.[8]

According to my hypothesis, women in philosophy are susceptible to experiencing a specific form of social alienation, which has been described as "a sense of incongruence" and "dissonance" by feminist critics (Allen et al. 2008, 164, 177, 185; Dotson 2012, 13–14). This alienation cannot be reduced to the inevitable alienation from the self, nor is it likely that it would be entirely tied to the economic system, considering that women have occupied a marginal position in philosophy ever since the days of Ancient Greece. With its ideology of constant competition and aspiration to produce more "results" with fewer resources, the recent educational politics has definitely made academic work increasingly precarious. Even so, it adds just an extra layer to the aforementioned sense of incongruence.

It is important to acknowledge that this alienation is not total. Philosophy as an art of thinking and as a possibility to ask fundamental questions is not what women students of philosophy and professional philosophers appear to feel alienated from. Should we then assume, following Hegel's second scenario, that philosophy *as a profession with specific social structures*—as distinct from to philosophy as radical

---

[7] At that point Hegel argued that in comparison to the religious life of Ancient Greece, the Christian religion of his time represented an empty and alienated cultural form, which its practitioners follow under pressure, without a free engagement that would make the religion living (see Taylor 180, 23–41).

[8] According Lacan, self-alienation is a necessary state for every human being, one that cannot be avoided: in its initial attempt to find its unity in the other, the self is fundamentally split. Sartre likewise argued that there is something profoundly dislocated in human existence, a fundamental gap between one's attempt to achieve a fixed identity and one's inability to stop the movement of transcendence. Finally, the same view of alienation as the permanent state of the human being can be found at the core of Derrida's philosophy (see Skempton 2010).

questioning and an art of thinking—has evolved past the phase in which it was the expression of the lives of its practitioners, and has become a hollow form which they no longer identify with? The problem is, of course, that the form may appear hollower to some than to others. Despite the fact that some women students and professional women philosophers adjust to the discipline without a problem, it may, indeed, be more typical of women than of men to seriously question the practices and limits of philosophy itself, for women were never the ones who primarily created those practices and limits. This imbalance is at the very core of the questions posed in this book.

References

Allen, Anita. 2008. Situated Voices: Black Women in/on the Profession of Philosophy. *Hypatia* 23 (2): 160–189.
Asher, Nina. 2003. Engaging Difference: Towards a Pedagogy of Interbeing. *Teaching Education* 14 (3): 235–247.
Beauvoir, Simone de. 1960. *La force de l'âge*. Paris: Gallimard. English edition: Beauvoir, Simone de. 1984. English edition: *The Prime of Life* (trans. Green, Peter). Harmondsworth, Middlesex, UK: Penguin Books.
Beauvoir, Simone de. 2008. *Le deuxième sexe II : L'expérience vécue*. Paris: Gallimard. English edition: Beauvoir, Simone de. 2010. *The Second Sex* (trans. Borde, Constance and Malovany-Chevallier, Sheila). New York, NY: Alfred A. Knopf.
Bolger, Meg. 2018. Why I Don't Facilitate Privilege Walks Anymore and What I Do Instead. https://medium.com/@MegB/why-i-dont-won-t-facilitate-privilege-walks-anymore-and-what-i-do-instead-380c95490e10. Accessed 4 April 2022.
Caporale-Bizzini, Silvia and Melita Richter Malabotta (eds). 2009. *Teaching Subjectivity: Travelling Selves for Feminist Pedagogy*. Teaching with Gender. Utrecht: ATHENA3.
Christine, de Pizan. 1999. *The Book of the City of Ladies*. Trans. Rosalind Brown-Grant. London: Penguin Books.
Dotson, Kristie. 2012. How is this Paper Philosophy? *Comparative Philosophy* 3 (1): 3–29. http://scholarworks.sjsu.edu/cgi/viewcontent.cgi?article=1039&context=comparativephilosophy. Accessed 22 April 2022.
Du Bois, W E B. 1964. *The Souls of Black Folk: Essays and Sketches*. Greenwich, CT: Fawcett.
Freire, Paulo. 1972. *Pedagogy of the Oppressed*. Trans. Myra Bergman Ramos. London: Sheed and Ward.
Gouldner, Alvin W. 1980. *The Two Marxisms: Contradictions and Anomalies in the Development of Theory*. London: Macmillan.
Hartsock, Nancy C. M. 1998. *The Feminist Standpoint Revisited and Other Essays*. Boulder, CO: Westwiew.
Haug, Frigga et al. 1987. *Female Sexualization: A Collective Work of Memory*. Trans. Erica Carter. London: Verso.
Hill Collins, Patricia. 2009. *Black Feminist Thought: Knowledge, Consciousness, and the Politics of Empowerment*. Routledge Classics. New York: Routledge.
hooks, bell. 1994. *Teaching to Transgress: Education as the Practice of Freedom*. New York: Routledge.
Kruks, Sonia. 1998. Beauvoir: The Weight of Situation. In *Simone de Beauvoir: A Critical Reader*, ed. Elizabeth Fallaize, 43–71. New York: Routledge. Originally published in Kruks, Sonia 1990. *Situation and Human Existence: Freedom, Subjectivity and Society*, 83–112. London: Unwin.

References

Lukács, Georg. 1975. *The Young Hegel: Studies in the Relations between Dialectics and Economics.* London: Merlin Press.
Luke, Carmen and Jennifer Gore. 1992. *Feminisms and Critical Pedagogy.* New York, NY: Routledge.
Macaulay, Catharine. 2014. *Letters on Education: With Observations on Religious and Metaphysical Subjects.* Cambridge: Cambridge University Press.
Onyx, Jenny and Jennie Small. 2001. Memory-Work: The Method. *Qualitative Inquiry,* 7 (6), 773–786.
Radomska, Marietta. 2013. Posthuman Pedagogies: Toward an Ethics of the Non/Living. *Journal of Curriculum and Pedagogy*: 28–31.
Rautio, Pauliina and Päivi Jokinen. 2016. Childrens Relations to the More-than-Human World Beyond Developmental Views. In *Play and Recreation, Health and Wellbeing,* eds Bethan Evans, John Horton and Tracey Skelton, 35–47. Singapore: Springer.
Ruonakoski, Erika. 2015. Interdisciplinarity in *The Second Sex*: Between Phenomenology and Psychoanalysis. In *Simone de Beauvoir—A Humanist Thinker,* eds Tove Pettersen ja Annlaug Bjørsnøs, 41–56. Leiden: Brill.
Ruonakoski, Erika. 2017. Retranslating *The Second Sex* into Finnish: Choices, Practices, and Ideas. In *On ne naît pas femme : on le devient: The Life of a Sentence,* eds Bonnie Mann and Martina Ferrari, 31–54. New York, NY: Oxford University Press.
Sanson, Megan, Deryn Strange and Maryanne Garyn. 2019. Trigger Warnings Are Trivially Helpful for Reducing Negative Affect, Intrusive Thoughts, and Avoidance. *Clinical Psychological Science* 7 (4), 778–793.
Sartre, Jean-Paul. 2003. *Being and Nothingness: An Essay on Phenomenological* Ontology. Trans. Hazel E. Barnes. London: Routledge.
Schalk, Meike, Thérèse Kristiansson and Ramia Mazé. 2017. *Feminist Futures of Spatial Practice: Materialisms, Activisms, Dialogues, Pedagogies, Projections.* Baunach: AADR—Art Architecture Design Research & Spurbuch.
Simons, Margaret A. 1999. "Richard Wright, Simone De Beauvoir, and the Second Sex." In *Beauvoir and the Second Sex: Feminism, Race, and the Origins of Existentialism,* ed. Margaret A. Simons, 167–184. Lanham: Rowman & Littlefield Publishers.
Skempton, Simon. 2010. *Alienation After Derrida.* London: Bloomsbury.
Taylor, Mark C. 1980. *Journeys to Selfhood: Hegel & Kierkegaard.* Berkeley: University of California Press.
Thompson, Becky. 2017. *Teaching with Tenderness: Toward an Embodied Practice.* Urbana, IL: University of Illinois Press.
Wollstonecraft, Mary. 2000. *A Vindication of the Rights of Women.* South Bend: Infomations.

Open Access This chapter is licensed under the terms of the Creative Commons Attribution 4.0 International License (http://creativecommons.org/licenses/by/4.0/), which permits use, sharing, adaptation, distribution and reproduction in any medium or format, as long as you give appropriate credit to the original author(s) and the source, provide a link to the Creative Commons license and indicate if changes were made.

The images or other third party material in this chapter are included in the chapter's Creative Commons license, unless indicated otherwise in a credit line to the material. If material is not included in the chapter's Creative Commons license and your intended use is not permitted by statutory regulation or exceeds the permitted use, you will need to obtain permission directly from the copyright holder.

Chapter 3
The Historical Situation

Abstract How does the history of philosophy affect the situation of women students in the field today and how has that situation changed over the years? From the very early days of philosophy, there have been women with either indirect or direct access to philosophical education. The fact that women are interested in philosophy and want to study it has received some attention even in the texts attributed to ancient philosophers, such as Plato and Phintys. However, ever since those days, women have remained a minority within philosophy and their position in it has been fairly precarious. To analyse the perpetuation of women's marginalisation in philosophy, I introduce Le Dœuff's idea of the erotico-theoretical transference and discuss the cult of genius. In addition, I scrutinise the temporal and pedagogical meaning of having women predecessors in philosophy, and suggest ways of integrating such predecessors in the curriculum. The chapter ends with the goals and outcomes of a related experimental summer school titled Feminist Thinking in Historical Perspective.

3.1 The Historical Roots of Women's Inclusion and Alienation in Philosophy

The discussion on women's philosophising started in ancient Greece. Some passages in Plato's *Republic* (fourth century BCE), are the best-known example, but, interestingly, a fragment of text attributed to the ancient woman philosopher Phintys takes a stand on the issue:

> While many people perhaps think that it is not appropriate for a woman to philosophise, just as it is not appropriate for her to ride horses nor to speak in public, I think that some activities are peculiar to men, some to women, and that some are common to women and men, some are more appropriate for men than women, and some are more appropriate for women than men.[1] (Phintys, translation I. A. Plant in Plant 2004, 85).

Even though the larger whole of the extant fragment leaves the author's conclusion of the right relationship between women and philosophising somewhat open, the text

---

[1] The original Greek text can be found in Johannes Stobaeus's *Anthologie* 4.23.61; 4.23.61a.

is usually interpreted as an early defence of women's access to philosophy. While the identity and even the gender of the author remain uncertain, this text demonstrates that the question of women's philosophical capacities and whether they should learn it was discussed quite early in the history of philosophy, in this case possibly in the third century BCE.[2]

Philosophy was practised and learnt predominantly by upper-class males and prospective leaders of Graeco-Roman Antiquity, but some philosophical schools, such as the Pythagoreans or Plato's Academy, did accept female members. As it is well known, Socrates argues in *The Republic* that as different natures are distributed evenly among men and women, also women should be able to become guardians (455e), and the same things should be taught to men and women (451e). In reality, women's philosophical education could not be taken for granted. Sometimes women came to enjoy this education indirectly, through their family members,[3] and many of the women philosophers of Antiquity were, in fact, wives and daughters of male philosophers (see e.g. Castner 1982). Of some female students Diogenes Laertius writes that they dressed as men, in order to escape becoming hetairas (DL 3.1.46).

Not all students of philosophy were from the upper class: Epicurus is said to have been joined in his philosophical studies by Mys, a person he enslaved (DL 10.3), and for some philosophical schools, such as the Cynics, poverty was an ideal, which led some members to give away their fortune. Of the Stoic philosophers, Epictetus (55–135 CE) was, in fact, originally an enslaved person, who later obtained his freedom and founded a philosophical school.

The role of women is described in a fairly similar manner in the few extant texts attributed to ancient Greek women philosophers, all Pythagoreans (Theano, Perictione, Phintys, Melissa, Aesara, and Myia), as well as in many of the Greek male philosophers' texts. It is debated whether this is because the views of male and female philosophers are actually similar or because the texts attributed to women were

---

[2] There is very little reliable information about the ancient Greek female philosophers, but allegedly Phintys was a Spartan-born female philosopher, who lived as a member of a Pythagorean community in Italy. According to Kathleen Wider (1986), she lived in the third century BCE. Mary B. Fant and Maureen B. Lefkowitz argue that the text was in fact written as a rhetorical exercise by a later male Pythagorean, and that it was erroneously attributed to Phintys, an earlier female philosopher (Fant and Lefkowitz 1982, 208n). Mary Ellen Waithe, however, accepts Stobaeus's claim that Phintys was a fifth century philosopher and actually wrote the fragment attributed to her (1987, 73). Whichever the case, the author's differentiation between what is appropriate, what is common and what is peculiar or natural leads the author to state that intellect and courage are common to both women and men, whereas they are more natural to men, and moderation is more natural to women. The fragment does not tell us much about the author's conclusion on women and philosophy, but it can be deduced that the author links philosophising with the virtue of intelligence. In other words, philosophising may not be as natural to women as it is to men, but it is not inappropriate for women to philosophise. In accordance with the Pythagorian teachings, the author appears to insinuate that a philosophical education helps women to attain their greatest virtue, namely moderation (*sophrosyne*), which was one of the Greek cardinal virtues. Aspiring to this virtue appears to be reconcilable with philosophising, which is why philosophising is appropriate for women.

[3] The Cynic philosopher Hipparchia (350–280 BCE), for instance, accessed philosophy first through her brother, who attended a philosophical school, and only later got to know the Cynic philosopher Crates, who subsequently became her husband. See DL 6.7.96–98.

written pseudonymously by male philosophers.[4] According to the text attributed to Phintys, it is particular to a woman to keep house, stay indoors and look after her husband, while the vilest thing she can do is to mix "with men outside the family" and to give birth to "bastards". In contrast to this, men's natural tendencies, political activity and public speaking, cannot be reduced to loyalty to their wives or family. Apart from the case of Hipparchia (350–280 BCE), who abandoned all comforts of life to live with Crates in the streets in the way of the Cynics, and Aspasia of Miletus (c. 470–410 BCE), who is depicted in conflicting ways but appears to have had a lot of influence in her time, most anecdotes about ancient women philosophers as well as the handful of remaining texts attributed to women would place them in a docile and self-effacing outgroup. Even in Plato's utopia, where philosopher women do not confine themselves to childrearing and housekeeping activities, these women are "handed over" to the men philosophers to produce new individuals of excellence (*Rep.* 458c, 459d). According to Plato, Socrates also claims that women are weaker than men in everything they do (*Rep.* 451e, 455d–e).

It should be noted, however, that even though the extant fragments attributed to women philosophers are scarce, this does not mean that some of the ancient women philosophers would not have been influential and well-respected in their own time. According to a contemporary historian, the astronomer, mathematician and Neoplatonist philosopher Hypatia (355–415 CE), whose writings have not survived to our days, made "such attainments in literature and science, as to far surpass all the philosophers of her own time".[5]

It would seem, then, that while it is not impossible for a woman to attain a high status in of the community of philosophers, women as a group have remained on the margins. From this perspective, it is hardly surprising that Pythagoras's philosophical school—which allowed female members—was, in fact, called a brotherhood. In the case of this particular school, the connotation of religious orders or secret brotherhoods is not totally mistaken, as it had a leaning towards mysticism and entering it required participating in a rite of initiation. Yet the idea of brotherly interaction or even rivalry is not far removed from, for example, Plato's dialogues, be it as it may that Socrates's superior position remains largely unchallenged.

It can still be asked why philosophy has maintained the form of a fairly homosocial and ethnically homogenous community. After all, many fields that used to be male-dominated, such as medicine, are no longer so, and even riding horses[6] and speaking

---

[4] In Melissa's (third century BCE) letter to Clearata, the author emphasises the importance for women to act moderately and to obey their husbands, which is why the letter has been suspected of being written pseudonymously by a male author (Plant 2004, 81). In contrast, even if the text attributed to Myia was hardly written by Theono's and Pythagoras's daughter Myia (c. 500 BCE), it would seem to be written by a woman, given the detailed descriptions of breastfeeding and advice on how to choose a nurse for a baby (Plant 2004, 79–80).

[5] Socrates of Constantinople: *Ecclesiastical History*. Even if the ancient Greek culture does appear rather restrictive of women's space in society, female poets, such as Sappho and Anyte, were spoken of admiringly in the works male authors (see e.g. Meleager, *AP* 4.1).

[6] In countries such as Sweden, France and the United States, the overwhelming majority of riders are nowadays women (Hedenborg 2007; Lagier 2009; White 2003).

in public, mentioned in Phintys's text as quite inappropriate for women, have become perfectly acceptable for women in Western countries, at least for now. What appears to differentiate philosophy from these activities, however, is the persistence of its masculine stamp.

The question then arises: are women as a group simply incompetent or generally uninterested in philosophy? I would argue that there is nothing inherently gendered about the practice of philosophy as wonder, doubt, dialogue, critique, and a shared quest for truth and wisdom. As long as philosophy operates in this mode, it holds a promise of the freedom and power of thought and appears valuable to those who appreciate these things. In other words, I disagree with those who argue that, as a conceptual discipline, philosophy is inherently misogynist. Another aspect of philosophy, however, is related to a claim for ownership of knowledge, expertise and authority. In this game those, who feel more insecure about their entitlement to be heard, can have difficulties in getting recognition for their own points of departure and interests. As we will see, Le Dœuff argues that the perpetuation of women's marginality in philosophy depends on the idea of the philosopher as someone who possesses knowledge.

3.2 The Perpetuation of Women's Marginality

In *The Philosophical Imaginary*, Le Dœuff proposes a psychoanalytic discussion on the development of women's position in the history of philosophy. She argues that due to their long-lasting exclusion from academia, women failed to develop an independent relationship to philosophy. Typically, a woman's love for theory was transferred to a male philosopher, who adopted the role of a teacher, to the extent that the woman's relationship to philosophy was totally mediated by that one philosopher. This shift is what she calls "erotico-theoretical transference" (Le Dœuff 1989, 104).[7] In the spirit of, Hipparchia (350–280 BCE) married her teacher Crates (365–285 BCE), Héloïse (c. 1098–1164) was associated with her teacher Abelard (1079–1142), Elisabeth, Princess of Bohemia (1618–1680) with René Descartes (1596–1650), and even Beauvoir (1908–1986), who already had an access to university education, with a student slightly her senior, Sartre (1905–1980) (See Le Dœuff 1989, 100–120).

Le Dœuff insists that it is not the presence of women students that diverts the master–disciple relationship towards the instinctive realm, nor is the discussed transference only the product of women's historical exclusion from universities. Rather, philosophical didactics itself "tends to take the form of a dual transference relationship". According to LeDœuff, male students of philosophy are also likely to experience their own version of the erotico-theoretical transference, to the extent that they may emulate the clothing styles of the object of their admiration (Le Dœuff 1989, 105–106).

---

[7] For a detailed discussion of Le Dœuff's ideas and a comparison between them and Luce Irigaray's philosophy, see Lehtinen (2007).

3.2 The Perpetuation of Women's Marginality

Le Dœuff argues, however, that in the past centuries, women's relationship to philosophy was characterised by a different form of lack than men's. After becoming disappointed with their advisors, men students of philosophy came to realise that their lack is of the radical kind that the Other cannot complete. This philosophical lack is the true starting point of philosophy and leads them to new questions, a re-evaluation of the philosophical tradition, and new ideas. For women students, who were only amateurs, being shut outside universities, the situation became problematic. Their lack remained of the ordinary kind, that can be fulfilled by the all-knowing master (Le Dœuff 1989, 105–107).

In Le Dœuff's view, the desire of a student can be redirected towards theory and the whole field of philosophy only within the institutional framework. She argues that even now, when women students can, in principle, enjoy the same institutional support as men, they still move very prudently within philosophy, carefully examining the work of past philosophers, often conforming with the demands of the academic life to every detail. At the same time, they have difficulties in performing as the possessors of true knowledge, which is something that, according to Le Dœuff, still characterises the role of the philosopher. Nevertheless, she argues that rather than criticise women's ways of doing philosophy, we should give up the ideal of philosophy that leaves no room for lack of knowledge. She also suggests that the subject of philosophy should not be seen so much as a master who knows, a solitary all-knowing subject. Instead, we could see philosophy as a collective enterprise which leaves space for not-knowing (Le Dœuff 1989, 116–127).

Le Dœuff undoubtedly exaggerates the extent to which the relationship of women philosophers to philosophy was mediated through their lovers, and how derivative their thinking was. Even if Le Dœuff's description of this relationship was read loosely as a description of falling in love with philosophy without being able to transcend the mediating role of one male philosopher, rather than as descriptions of clearly erotic relationships between individuals, it can be argued that she overlooks the diversity of women's relationships to their advisors. In cases like those of Hypatia, Christine de Pizan (1364–1430) and Lucrezia Marinella (1571–1653), the father's role was important, and one can only assume that the encouragement of a father can have a function rather different from that of a lover, a husband or even a distantly admired teacher. Possibly the father's appreciation and support for the daughter's intellectual endeavours could strengthen her self-esteem and facilitate her entrance into a male-dominated field. Close relationships with fathers and brothers could also initiate women in the tacit rules of social interaction between men. Even Le Dœuff's paradigmatic example, Hipparchia, was not only Crates's lover but had entered philosophy through her brother.[8]

Respectively, the difficulty of women to enter the field of philosophy could partly be explained more simply than by Le Dœuff's hypothesis of different kinds of desires, namely by the aspect of homosociality within the field. On the basis of this homosociality hypothesis, in a group that consists of mainly individuals of one gender, the behavioural patterns of that gender would tend to become the norm, whereas the

---

[8] DL 6.7.96–98.

individuals of the minority would feel a pressure to adapt to the norm. In the case of women philosophy students and professional women philosophers, this would imply assimilating the role of the "good guy". One's ability and willingness to take on this role would then predict social success and continuation in the field whereas an inability or unwillingness to adhere to the norm would predict alienation and opting out. On the other hand, homosociality as the more or less unconscious desire to bond with individuals of the same gender rather than with other genders could also explain how the boundaries of philosophy are at the same time porous and resistant. Depending on the situation and the proportion of women among the participants, the tacit rules of interaction can vary a great deal, and hence women's experiences of inclusion can likewise vary a great deal within the same community.

In any case, Le Dœuff's conclusion about the needed transformation is sound. For the practice of philosophy to become more inclusive and, in fact, more philosophical, philosophy should be seen more in terms of a continuously evolving process of thought rather than as mastery. Young women become enthralled by the open-ended quest that philosophy purports to be in the first instance, but many of them experience discomfort when they realise that in order to "make it" in philosophy, they have to fight for speaking space and repeatedly demonstrate their learnedness, argumentative skills and possession of knowledge. From their perspective there is something self-defeating in the philosophical enterprise: it promises dialogue and freedom of thought but often produces hierarchies and silencing.

In what follows, I examine the role of the philosophical canon and a phenomenon connected closely to it, namely the cult of the genius, in learning philosophy. The problem of this aspect of philosophy will be analysed in some detail. I start my discussion from the more rewarding side of being in a relationship to the canon, namely the patient labour of thinking with the other that philosophy students are encouraged to pursue.

3.3 Dealing with the Tradition: Intimacy and Idolatry

In philosophy, more than in many other fields, the tradition is mediated through a discussion of a canon, that is, texts from the history of philosophy that are deemed central or epoch-making. That the canon is quite homogenous in terms of the gender and ethnicity of the authors is a question that has been implicitly present in the preceding considerations of women's marginality. This phenomenon is connected to another equally problematic one, the cult of the genius. I argue that the mediation of the tradition through canonical texts is not merely problematic but can be seen as one of the distinctive features of philosophy. That we might need to allow for a plurality of canons does not imply that we should or could cut the ties of philosophy with its past. Philosophy involves a dialogue across millennia, and in its ability to provide a link to historical others it resembles some other disciplines, such as literature studies or history. What is specific to philosophy, however, is the role that the texts and their authors take. Even though a study of those texts produces information about their

3.3 Dealing with the Tradition: Intimacy and Idolatry

authors and their intellectual context, very often philosophers are motivated by the possibilities of dialogue and of obtaining a better understanding of issues that the historical philosopher discusses.

In the process of reading and studying the texts, the authors become important interlocutors to the readers, be the latter students or researchers. As I have argued elsewhere, following Beauvoir, there is a specific intimacy to the reading experience: the other—the author, the narrator, the text—speaks to the person reading, and yet the reader is the one who acts to bring these words to life. Indeed, a particular kind of intersubjectivity exists within the reading experience, one that involves both passivity and activity on the part of the reader: the words written by the other guide the reader's attention and take the place of one's own "inner speech", yet without the act of reading and the reader's own imaginative input the letters would remain mere black marks on white background. In other words, while reading, we adopt the voice of the other as our own, sharing, in part, its intentionality. At the same time, the voice of the other remains foreign to us: it speaks to us within us, activated by us, but the only control we exert over it is the control over starting and ceasing to read (See Korhonen and Ruonakoski 2017, 30–33, and Beauvoir 1965, 1979, 2011a and 2011b). Even so, we can disagree and pause to think of alternative ways of dealing with the issues the author is addressing. The alteration between the activity of reading and reflective pauses is, in fact, how the philosophical dialogue works during the reading process. Perhaps more than in the case of reading fiction, we engage in a movement between activating the words of the author, developing an affective stance on them—one of disbelief, acceptance or of a happy recognition—and pauses to formulate the beginnings of possible counterarguments.[9]

Indeed, philosophical writings are not read mainly because they provide "facts" but because they help us think by engaging both our affective and reflective abilities. It is a mistake to read Hannah Arendt because she tells us "facts" about how the Nazis came to power or even "facts" about the nature of the totalitarian; instead, one should read *The Origins of Totalitarianism* (1951/2017) in order to learn to think about totalitarianism with her. This is precisely the liberating aspect of reading

---

[9] Literary theorists typically distinguish the experience of reading literary fiction and more scholarly texts. From Aristotle's *Poetics* on, theorists have formulated in different ways the idea that, unlike scholarly texts, literary texts—or in Aristotle's case "mimetic" texts—are not expected to make arguments (see e.g. Beauvoir 2011a and 1979). Likewise, reading fiction is said to differ from reading scholarly texts because it involves participation in a multitude of different perspectives. I have argued that while these descriptions do point towards some important features of literature, the distinction between literary and other texts may not be altogether clear-cut. Even scholarly texts can involve something like successive perspective changes, when the author moves from discussing views of their own to those of others, and then returns to criticism or affirmation of the other's view (Korhonen and Ruonakoski 2017, 203n). A lot could be said about the possibility and nature of "inner speech" and about whether the reader's interlocutor should be described as the author, the implied author, the narrator, or the text as such, but within the framework of this book it is not possible to dwell on these issues. See, however, Merleau-Ponty's discussion on thought and expression (2012, 188–9; 1998, 212–14), Iser (1980) for a discussion of the act of reading, Niederhoff for a narratological discussion of perspective and focalisation (2011a, b), and Schmid (2013) for the question of the implied author.

philosophical works: not learning *what* to think but engaging critically in an inner dialogue with someone who has already produced an analysis of particular topic, learning *to* think with the other more rigorously and more creatively than you would be able to do all by yourself.

I have discussed the issue of reading philosophical works at some length in order to show how much feeling can be invested in this act, and what kind of liberating power it has. Yet there is a flipside to this affective–intellectual process: the author becomes the object of an adoration similar to fiction authors, and, with the institutional support to the philosophical canon, acquires the cloak of genius. In other words, the very human need to be in contact with another human on an intellectual level, together with the cultural demand for academic trailblazers as sources of inspiration, paradoxically contributes to the production of a demigod. Given the scarcity or virtual non-existence of women philosophers in the canon, this phenomenon is particularly problematic from the viewpoint of women students.

What do we then mean by "a genius"? To be sure, the meaning of the word has changed radically over time. Christine Battersby, the author of *Gender and Genius* (1989), argues that the current conception of the genius was born only in the eighteenth century, with the Romantics, when the two concepts of "genius" (Lat. *genius*) and "ingenious" (Lat. *ingenium*) amalgamated. In Roman Antiquity, the word *genius* first referred to a male household spirit, and it was associated with the *paterfamilias*, the male head of a household, but later each free male was considered to have from his birth a genius, which represented his potential virility and life-giving force. (Battersby 1989, 52–53). *Ingenium*, on the other hand, referred to natural abilities or inborn talent.

Skipping the intriguing gendered developments of these concepts through the Middle Ages and the Renaissance and entering the Age of Enlightenment, we come to see that Immanuel Kant conflated the concepts in his influential *The Critique of Judgement* (1790; see Battersby 1989, 76): "*Genius* is the innate mental aptitude (*ingenium*) *through which* nature gives the rule to art" (2007, 136, §46).[10] Kant underlines that genius is a natural gift, a talent that differs from dexterity (*Geschicklichkeitsanlage*), which was, according to Battersby, earlier associated with *ingenium*. For Kant, genius is opposite to the spirit of imitation and characterised primarily by originality (Kant 2007, §46–47; Battersby 1989, 43–51, 76–77). He is aware of the etymology the word, and describes the workings of the genius, as if nature itself worked through a man:

> Hence, where an author owes a product to his genius, he does not himself know how *the ideas* for it have entered into his head, nor has he it in his power to invent the like at pleasure, or methodically, and communicate the same to others in such precepts as would enable them to produce similar products (Kant 2007, 137, §46).

---

[10] The beginning of the German original of §46 reads as follows: "*Genie* ist das Talent (Naturgabe), welches der Kunst die Regel gibt. Da das Talent, als angebornes produktives Vermögen des Künstlers, selbst zur Natur gehört, so könnte man sich auch so ausdrücken: *Genie* ist die angeborne Gemütsanlage (ingenium), *durch welche* die Natur der Kunst die Regel gibt.".

3.3 Dealing with the Tradition: Intimacy and Idolatry

True enough, Kant discusses genius in the context of great art, but Arthur Schopenhauer, who proclaimed himself a Kantian (and a man of genius), discussed genius in a larger scope, as a category of superhumans. For Schopenhauer, geniuses were also characterised by solitude:

> The same reason indeed accounts for the peculiar inclination of all men of genius for solitude, to which they are driven by their difference from the rest, and for which their own inner wealth qualifies them. For, with humanity it is as with diamonds, the extraordinarily great ones alone are fitted to be solitaires, while those of ordinary size have to be set in clusters to produce any effect (Schopenhauer 1907, 251).[11]

In Schopenhauer's philosophy the celebration of the genius as a virile force, which nonetheless incorporates feminine sensitivities, is conflated with a clearly misogynist discussion of women's capacities (see Battersby 1989, 107–111). However, it is difficult to see how the category of the philosopher genius—which Schopenhauer and Friedrich Nietzsche[12] were perhaps the keenest to represent—could even in principle accommodate women, given that the Romantic idea of genius which we have inherited was built on the idea of male life-giving force. According to Battersby, it has often been the case that male thinkers have specifically argued against the possibility of the female genius (1989, 3–4).

Indeed, the idea of the solitary philosopher genius seems to accommodate poorly women thinkers and those of different minorities, who may fail to see themselves as legitimate heirs to the tradition. Occasionally one can witness among White male students a kind of affectionate mocking attitude towards the "big names" in philosophy, as if Aristotle and Heidegger were their big brothers who they make fun of but at the same time admire and feel supported by. Whether or not women philosophy students were likely to adopt a similar jocular attitude towards historical women thinkers, the very fact that these thinkers never occupied such a universally iconic position in the philosophical canon as the male philosophers makes for a nonparallel relationship: mocking historical women thinkers is hardly like mocking the incomparably ingenious and influential ancestor but rather like mocking the already ridiculed, poor and marginalised distant relative, a mad auntie who herself may be the only one to think that she is a philosopher.

In philosophy seminars, there exists a pressure to say something "smart" that demonstrates that you already have a good command of philosophy and that you are able ask the "right" kind of questions. It is difficult to say how much the varying ways in which students respond to the situation—from apparent arrogance to verbosity and refraining from speech—reflect their attempts to hide their uncertainties and the tacit expectations of the role of the philosopher. Yet for some of the women students these expectations and the general atmosphere of seminars may very well belong to the alienating aspects of philosophy.

---

[11] The English translation, *On the Fourfold Root of the Principle of Sufficient Reason and On the Will in Nature*, includes two essays, which were published in German under the titles *Über die vierfache Wurzel des Satzes vom zureichenden Grunde* (1813) and *Über den Willen in der Natur* (1836).

[12] According to Carl Pletsch, Nietzsche's life demonstrates that "genius is a role that needs to be learnt and nurtured" (1991, 15).

In the mythical imagination, the solitary hero philosopher is seen to sacrifice bourgeois comforts and even their own mental health for a rigorous pursuit of an inner truth, as manifested by the popularity of the legends of Schopenhauer's supposed dysthymia, Nietzsche's syphilis-related confusion, Ludwig Wittgenstein's tendency to depression and his entertainment of suicidal thoughts, or Simone Weil's supposed pseudo-anorexia (see e.g. Hannan 2009, Margulis 2004, Peters 2019, Oxenhandler 1994).[13] The idea of the philosopher as a lone wolf can be actually harmful, when it dominates the way students conceive their future possibilities and the most profitable actions. Philosophy majors may think that to be taken seriously or to achieve their own ideals, they should dedicate their lives to philosophy, that is, always put philosophy first and more mundane pursuits second. In reality, functioning relationships with their peers can be equally or more important for their ability to be creative in philosophy and to enjoy studying it.[14]

If this is the case, philosophy students who find support in like-minded peers or generous supervisors, will be more likely to feel "at home" in philosophy and less likely to let any difficulties send them off the rails. It takes a lot of determination to continue in a competitive field when there is neither social support nor financial reward in view. In addition, the idea of the philosopher's work as a solitary struggle can have repercussions for how professional philosophers act in the role of leaders and teachers.

If we are not happy with the idea of genius as it has been described above, should we then reject it altogether? Rejection of this idea may be easier said than done, for it cannot be denied that being recognised as beyond compare in one's field remains one of the alluring qualities of the genius, and ultimately, a ticket away from the seeming futility of existence.[15] In reality, though, attaining a high standard in one's field may not be so much a question of innate talent, as the Romantics would have had it, but one of practice and perseverance (see Berliner and Eyre 2018). Yet even perseverance is not enough, if you do not find the right people with whom to discuss and develop your ideas, and to support you—who help you flourish.

After all, the cult of genius obscures the character of philosophy as a collective endeavour and emphasises the person instead of the work. As is frequently repeated, philosophy is dialogue. We discuss ideas that belong to a tradition; we try to understand that tradition and the views of others as best we can even when we wish to

---

[13] While it is problematic to diagnose historical figures after their death, the described psychological problems, real or unreal, make an important part of the legends of these philosophers. Dysthymia refers to chronic depression, which may include feelings of hopelessness, fatigue and low self-esteem. Pseudo-anorexia is an eating disorder that a patient can develop in order to deny the reality of a supposedly more uncontrollable disease. Simone Weil is known to have refused to eat during her illness, which precipitated her death.

[14] To be able to say something more definitive about the matter, an empirical study would be in order. These considerations are based on my discussions with philosophy students, the background study for this volume and other unpublished surveys.

[15] In her introduction to *Genius: The History of an Idea*, Penelope Murray argues that a genius is generally understood to be an individual with exceptional gifts, who nonetheless differs from people who are simply talented (1989, 1).

3.3 Dealing with the Tradition: Intimacy and Idolatry

overcome that tradition. We also ask for our peers' comments and counterarguments for whatever new ideas we are able to develop. Philosophy is a collective effort in the sense that it requires a community of thinkers who believe in the importance of doing philosophy and who, across millennia, strive for clarity and a better understanding of reality. True enough, at the same time it is the effort of individuals, who often need solitude in order to engage in this dialogue with their full capacity and who enjoy working alone. In this context, what should we make of the category of genius?

Battersby's solution is not to discard genius altogether but to discard the Romantic idea of it as a solitary man, who resembles a "mad" person but at the same time embodies a virile force of life, and expresses utmost originality. In her view, the task of feminists is to change the definition of genius and to bring out women geniuses. And in fact, during a workshop in which the cult of genius was being discussed, a woman colleague exclaimed: "Don't we all want to be geniuses?" Perhaps this question could be transformed into the form: "Don't we all want to achieve individual brilliance in our thinking?" In that case, the answer is probably "yes". We do not do philosophy to be bad or mediocre thinkers, such as those inferior interlocutors of Socrates, who get it so wrong before he helps them out.

Brilliance is something that we can achieve in philosophy through a long and loving engagement in thinking, discussing and writing. Achieving it does not require being placed higher than others in the intellectual hierarchy, but rather succeeding in a more limited endeavour. From the perspective of temporality, the satisfactory moments of "achieving brilliance" in one's work are not the moments in which others applaud the finished work, for, from the philosopher's viewpoint, the work in question exists in those moments mainly as a past engagement. When the philosopher's living engagement with the topic has already ceased to exist, however, the readers may find a promise of their own future possibilities in the finished work.[16] For the author, the philosopher, the actual satisfaction comes in the moments of insight, often after a long period of seemingly going in circles or of inefficiency, or the moments of flow, when philosophical thinking seems relatively effortless and appears to hold a lot of promise: it opens up towards a limitless future. These moments can be shared with others, or they can appear as the outcome of inspiring conversations. To be sure, recognition of one's work is important, too, and in a positive scenario, it can re-enliven the work for the author. Often this recognition exists as a celebration of a work that has already been left behind by the philosopher and represents a gap between the author and the readers.

It may be helpful to analyse brilliance in philosophical writings precisely through their abilities to position us temporally. If a work opens up new possibilities for the reader, if it transforms their relationship to their own future, the work is likely to appear to the reader as brilliant. This way of understanding brilliance as a kind of transformative force is somewhat—but not completely—relativistic, because, depending on the reader, different works have this power, and even the same reader

---

[16] Again, my analysis of temporality and intersubjectivity relies on Beauvoir's discussion of them in *Pyrrhus and Cineas* (2003; 2004).

experiences the same work differently depending on when they read it. This implies that some flexibility could be inherent in the constitution of canons.

The analysis reveals that the relationship of philosophy students to the canon, or to the part of that canon that they choose to familiarise themselves with, consists of a specific intimacy brought about by the act of reading itself, a dialogue over time (the phenomenon of "thinking together"), and, in optimal cases, a new set of intellectual and experiential possibilities opened up by those works. I suggest that even if we may retain something of the Romantic conception of "genius" and even though the institutional solidification of a specific canon legitimises a conception of certain thinkers as heroic and superior, we should not ignore the future-opening aspect of different philosophers' work that contributes to their adoration through the thankfulness it inspires. To help students analyse their relationship to the canon rather than just live it prereflectively, their teachers should explicitly address all of these aspects of engaging with the tradition.

Perhaps precisely because the concept of genius has decreased in value over the past decades, we seem to have attained the situation in which a woman or a person of colour or a person belonging to a gender minority can be seen as "a genius". Even though it is difficult to raise anyone of one's contemporaries as a genius, many women philosophers – Judith Butler, Luce Irigaray, Martha Nussbaum—seem to have already reached a status which would allow them to be later viewed as "women geniuses", if their ideas are later deemed central to the narrative of the history of philosophy, and they are not written out of this, which has often been the fate of women philosophers. Many of the posthumanist thinkers are also women and may be fathomed to acquire this position someday.

Some philosophers, however, suggest that there are objective reasons why Aristotle is in the canon and others like Butler should not be. According to Donald Phillip Verene, for instance, there are actually only four important philosophers—Plato, Aristotle, Kant and Hegel—whose works the rest of Western philosophy only comments on and responds to (Verene 2018, 7). Philosophy that puts social criticism first and creates a "surrogate" canon of gender, race and ethnicity, would endanger the core of philosophy and give up imagination and history of philosophy for the benefit of politics. In comparison to Plato and Aristotle, thinkers such as Butler would fail to manifest a complexity of thought and "greatness"—they supposedly only have "one principal idea" (Verene 2018, 15).

It may very well be that the demand that a philosopher's work need be both deep and broad in scope for it to be accepted into the canon makes it quite impossible for contemporary academic philosophers to ever gain this acceptance, for in the current state of science politics, specialisation is mandatory. Even so, the work of Butler and other contemporary philosophers can hardly be reduced to "one principal idea". Regardless of the constitution of the future canon or canons, it should be clear that the discussion of the existing canon can be combined with a discussion of more alternative texts. In any case, it is rare that any philosopher would be simultaneously be an expert in Plato, Aristotle, Kant and Hegel, not to mention a wider canon, which means that for each of us, our understanding of the field always remains uneven, in some aspects thorough and in others superficial.

As I have suggested, historical philosophical texts, despite their problems, open up a future to their readers. In what follows, I consider yet another empowering potential of the past: the power of a historical "we". To this end, the next section deals with the role female predecessors in philosophy.

3.4 Why and How to Raise Awareness of Early Women Philosophers

The thoughts attributed to Phintys were not discussed in the beginning of this chapter by chance. Rather, this was a case of deliberately introducing a *possibility* of an early female voice in philosophy, despite the fact that little of the writings of Greek women philosophers has been preserved to posterity, that these philosophers do not belong to the philosophical canon, and that their ideas may not appear particularly progressive from the perspective of philosophers of our time. Phintys's case is not, of course, ideal from our perspective, as the authorship and dating of the text attributed to her remain unclear. Even so, the idea that there is a thinking, arguing woman early in the history of philosophy, and that these could be her words, rather than just words of female characters in male philosophers' writings or male philosophers' views about women, can be meaningful as such for many students and professionals in philosophy. Why? Not because of any feminine essence that all women would share, but because that woman has spoken from the position of a woman, who is also a philosopher and a member of a minority within her philosophical community.

In other words, we are dealing with the formation of a "we" in the historical continuum that reaches from Graeco-Roman Antiquity to our days and to the coming generations women philosophers, towards whom our own actions open up. True enough, not all women philosophers relate themselves primarily to this continuum, but for some a sense of it may help affirm their belief in themselves as philosophers: the history of philosophy is not simply the history of men philosophers, even though it is often presented as one.

More precisely, the sense of belonging does not emerge merely from arguments proposed by philosophers, for it matters from which positions those arguments are proposed. When Socrates writes that women, too, should get a philosophical education, if they show talent for philosophy, a woman reader may think: "A point well made, Socrates. You stood up for us!"—happy for his words, even though he (or Plato as the author of *The Republic*) also says that women are weaker in everything they do in comparison to men, as we can recall. When a woman writes that women, too, should be able to philosophise, a female reader may think: "Good for you, sister! You stood up for us!" While the "us" refers in both cases to "us women", Socrates's argument comes from the ranks of the privileged majority and concerns a minority, whereas a woman philosopher speaks about a group she belongs to. The difference then comes to concern the sense of agency: whether I, as a woman philosopher or as a female student of philosophy, am given some concessions by a male philosopher, or whether I participate in the formation of an awareness of "us women" as agents of philosophising and of political questioning. What is more, it is relevant that through my own actions, I myself participate in achieving a goal that was recognised already by my female predecessors in the history of philosophy. In other words, it is not a question of merely achieving a goal but of participating in an action that makes the achievement of that goal possible (See Beauvoir 1948, 80; 2004a, 183–184).[17]

It would thereby seem important to raise awareness of early women philosophers. They can act as role models to women students and provide a fuller sense of what it is to be a practitioner of philosophy as a part of a continuum: I, as the subject experiencing both pleasure and difficulties in philosophy, am not alone—there have been others before me, and for them, too, these issues have had significance. When my female predecessors speak about the position of women in philosophy, I recognise a "we", rather than myself as an object of gaze and a historical male figure as its subject.

The attempt to raise awareness of female predecessors, however, immediately faces several obstacles. First of all, in the case of the earliest history of women philosophers, it is impossible to deny the scarcity of the remaining texts. In the case of ancient Greek philosophy, it may even be difficult to say whether the person to whom a text has been attributed, actually wrote it, as we saw for Phintys. Attempts to introduce the work of later women philosophers are complicated by the lack of available modern editions and translations. Secondly, it can be difficult to define the philosophical weight of some of these texts, especially if they are very short. Thirdly, the existing philosophical all-male canon is already in itself so dense that it is an impossible task for any contemporary philosopher to master all of it. Why introduce minor figures whose philosophy most certainly has been less influential than the existing canonical texts? Fourth, even if a philosopher who is not specialised in the history of women thinkers would like to introduce them on a course, this may be difficult to do without a degree of dilettantism. Finally, if we widen our horizons beyond the Northern hemisphere, to include African, Asian and South American philosophers, or philosophers of different minorities, does not our task of teaching philosophy become even more impossible and can it not at best provide only a very superficial glimpse into different philosophies rather than a solid understanding of the history of one?

Introducing some diversity in the curriculum need not, of course, lead to the exclusion of major European philosophers. It might not be a bad idea to broaden our views of what philosophy is. This diversification of course content could include both bringing new perspectives into individual courses and introducing whole courses with new content. To alleviate the problem of dilettantism, many sources on women philosophers exist already.

---

[17] In a similar way, Beauvoir emphasises the sense of agency in the liberation of Paris in 1944: "the goal was not a liberated of Paris, it was the liberation itself". In other words, it was pivotal for the participants to participate in the liberation rather than just being handed over a liberated city (Beauvoir 1948, 80; 2004a, 183–184).

3.4 Why and How to Raise Awareness of Early Women Philosophers

Authoring a monograph on the entire history of women philosophers for classroom use, is, of course, extremely challenging. I will just mention Mary Ellen Waithe's four-volume *A History of Women Philosophers* (1987, 1989, 1991, 1995), Cecile T. Tougas's and Sara Ebenreck's *Presenting Women Philosophers* (2000), Marit Rullmann's *Philosophinnen I und II* (1998a, b) and Ursula I. Meyer's *Philosophinnen-Lexikon* (1997). As regards books with a narrower focus on philosophers of a certain era or even individuals, certain topics and periods are better represented than others. For instance, a remarkable body of work exists on early modern women philosophers' treatises pertaining to epistemology and metaphysics. A lot has been written on the work of Elisabeth of Bohemia, Anne Conway, Margaret Cavendish, Émilie du Châtelet and Mary Wollstonecraft. Like male philosophers such as Descartes and Kant, these women philosophers have already been critically researched in detail and in what can be called interpretative traditions. In other words, it is no longer only a case of making these women philosophers' work known, but passing on ways of interpreting them to future generations.

Another question is how to integrate a discussion of women thinkers into the discussion of the male-dominated philosophical canon. There are several ways to tackle this issue. In teaching the history of philosophy, integration can be promoted minimally by giving references to the work of women philosophers or including some of their work in the reading materials, so that interested students can do at least part of their coursework on it. A more developed form of integrating historical women philosophers into teaching is discussing their work in conjunction with that of their male contemporaries, pointing out connections and actual dialogues between them. Finally, a deeper knowledge of work of the historical women philosophers may lead us to a new conception of the whole history of philosophy, and to the presentation of this history in a new way to the students.

There are already some online resources, from which we can draw when we plan inclusive teaching on different philosophical topics. Project Vox, for instance, showcases early modern women philosophers such as Cavendish (1623–1673), Conway (1631–1679), Damaris Cudworth Masham (1659–1708), Mary Astell (1666–1731) and Châtelet (1706–1749), providing alternative syllabi for discussing issues pertinent to philosophy of that era.[18] Another interesting resource is Extending New Narratives in the History of Philosophy, which provides links to several databases, and develops projects of its own, such as digitalising manuscripts of women philosophers.[19] The website Querelle publishes the pro-woman texts of the so-called *querelle des femmes*, particularly the work of sixteenth- and seventeenth-century Italian and French thinkers.[20] The German website History of Women Philosophers and Scientists offers information about historical women philosophers, their work and events related to them.[21]

---

[18] http://projectvox.org/. Accessed 21 April 2022.
[19] https://www.newnarrativesinphilosophy.net/index.html. Accessed 21 April 2022.
[20] http://querelle.ca/. Accessed 21 April 2022.
[21] https://historyofwomenphilosophers.org. Accessed 21 April 2022.

At the same time, the inclusion of women authors in the curriculum should not be reduced to historical figures. Inclusive teaching could also come to mean that whatever topic we deal with in our classes, we aim for gender balance in the reading materials. This is, in fact, more or less the practice in some universities—at the time of writing this work, for instance, at the University of Iceland. If all of the articles on our reading lists are written by men, we should consider the possibility that this does not reflect the actual gender balance of the writers of high-quality articles in that area, but that an implicit bias may be operating in our thinking, or that our interests are, in fact, gendered (see Haslanger 2008).

Most importantly, university teaching staff and researchers themselves are predecessors of the students, and whether they like it or not, often serve as role models. For women students and students belonging to other minorities in philosophy, the diversity of the staff is one positive signal that they could have a professional career in philosophy (see e.g. Dotson 2012). Molly Paxton, Carrie Fidgor and Valerie Tiberius have demonstrated that the presence of women lecturers on a philosophy course correlates with the percentage of women students. Yet it remains uncertain whether this correlation reflects the ability of female staff to cater for their women students' interests or whether their mere presence inspires women in their studies (Paxton et al. 2012).

3.5 The Jyväskylä Summer School: Feminist Thinking in Historical Perspective

The Jyväskylä Summer School was designed by Martina Reuter. A good proportion of the forty-one participants of the summer school came from the Erasmus + partnership universities. Some came also from other European countries and North America. 88% of the students were women.

The summer school was an experiment in how to integrate women thinkers into discussion of the history of philosophy in a novel and potentially empowering manner, creating different layers of dialogue through the ages and in the classroom. At the same time, the summer school proposed a nuanced critique of the politics of exclusion. It drew attention to how women thinkers have been excluded from the philosophical canon, but also to how feminist forerunners tend to be excluded from feminist canons.

The programme of this summer school was developed in a close interaction between the responsible lecturers, namely Reuter, Sandrine Bergès and Marguerite Deslauriers, who were all specialists in the history of philosophy. Together they had planned a course that would elucidate the development of feminist thought both as a part of the history of philosophy and in dialogue with the influential philosophers of each era. Starting from Plato and Aristotle, the lecturers went on to discuss the ideas of Héloïse, Christine de Pizan, Marie de Gournay, Lucrezia Marinella, Mary Astell, Poulain de la Barre, Jean-Jacques Rousseau, Madame Roland, Olympe de Gouges,

Mary Wollstonecraft and Simone de Beauvoir. Together with the reading materials, which included texts from the above-mentioned thinkers as well as articles on the feminist theory of the history of philosophy, the lectures provided a comprehensive introduction to the roots of feminist thought. The lecturers demonstrated how female and male thinkers had argued both with and against prominent philosophers such as Aristotle and Rousseau to defend feminist positions, and how ideas, which would not necessarily strike us as feminist, had contributed to the historical development of feminist modes of thinking.

In this course, the content was designed very carefully to provide a coherent narrative, and students were given a history against which they could reflect upon their own situation in philosophy. Importantly, they were given an overview of the ideas of early feminist thinkers, and a description of why and how these thinkers, whose intellectual background differed in a number of ways from ours and who thereby sometimes defended positions alien to us, could still be considered as feminists: they stood up for women and women's opportunities for action in their own societies, discussing the relationship between gender and power. In this way, the course not only provided the participants with a history of feminist thought, but also a wide, non-judgemental understanding of the possibilities of argumentation in a specific historical situation.

Pedagogically, the course was an example of how to discuss the history of philosophy creatively rather than following the established patterns. At the same time, this course demonstrated how one can, within fairly traditional modes of teaching such as lectures and reading seminars, still foster feelings of belonging and in fact empower students, when the content of the course is planned to support this. As Brook J. Sadler has pointed out, it is indeed possible to create a dialogical atmosphere through the careful elaboration of how the discussed philosophers have engaged in dialogue with each other (2004). This provides a model of dialogue for the students. In addition, the lecturer is an example of a philosopher engaging in a dialogue with other philosophers over time. Yet another level of dialogue is the dialogue between the students and the lecturer. Evidently the passion that the lecturer demonstrates for her topic and for the dialogue is also extremely important. When the lecturer demonstrates an affective relationship to the topic, it is easier for the student to be drawn towards that topic. In the course feedback, many of the students did in fact refer positively to the passion of the lecturers towards their topics.

A typical summer school day consisted of two 90-min lectures and a workshop, in which the students discussed the reading material of the day. The students were divided into three groups with three different instructors, due to the large number of participants. These seminar sessions were yet another opportunity for dialogue, which was more student-driven than during the lectures. At the end of the course—and following the model of the Icelandic summer school (see Sect. 4.4)—the students presented their research questions for the final papers in four groups. These groups were divided according to their topics, namely (1) concepts of gender, (2) equality and difference, (3) virtue and morality and (4) reason and passion. In a concluding session, students were asked to air their views about the summer school. After this summer school, like after all the others, the students were also asked to give feedback through a questionnaire.

Despite the generally positive undertone of the feedback, some participants found the course too Eurocentric. According to another criticism, the attempt to accommodate more than two thousand years of philosophy and feminist thinking within one course was overly ambitious. Perhaps this goes to show that the problem of exclusion and inclusion in presentation does not concern only the history of philosophy in general but also feminist thought. While many of the teaching staff may sigh at this point and think that we are facing an impossible mission, given that the expertise of one person can go only so far, this is not a reason to give up. Without claiming that there should no longer be courses in exclusively European philosophy, I suggest we acknowledge that the phase of globalisation we are living in right now could in fact produce new kinds of combinations in teaching and learning, and that increasing cooperation between feminist scholars from different parts of the world is a promising avenue to explore.

References

Arendt, Hannah. 2017. *The Origins of Totalitarianism*. London: Penguin Books.
Battersby, Christine. 1989. *Gender and Genius: Towards a Feminist Aesthetics*. London: Women's Press.
Beauvoir, Simone de. Idéalisme moral et réalisme politique. 1948. In *L'existentialisme et la sagesse des nations*, 54–102. Paris: Éditions Nagel. English edition: Beauvoir, Simone de. 2004a. Moral Idealism and Political Realism. In *Philosophical Writings*, eds Margaret A. Simons with Marybeth Timmermann and Mary Beth Mader, trans. Anne Deing Cordero, 175–193. Urbana, IL: University of Illinois Press.
Beauvoir, Simone de. 1965. Que peut la littérature? Intervention. In *Que peut la littérature?* ed. Yves Buin, 73–92. Paris: L'inédit 10/18. English edition: Beauvoir, Simone de. 2011b. What Can Literature do? In *"The Useless Mouths" and Other Literary Writings*, eds Margaret Simons and Marybeth Timmermann, trans. Marybeth Timmermann, 197–209. Urbana, IL: University of Illinois Press.
Beauvoir, Simone de. 1979. Mon experience d'écrivain. In *Les écrits de Simone de Beauvoir*, eds Claude Francis and Fernande Gautier, 439–57. Paris: Gallimard. English edition: Beauvoir, Simone de. My Experience as a Writer. 2011a. In *"The Useless Mouths" and Other Literary Writings*, eds Margaret A. Simons and Marybeth Timmermann, trans. Debbie J. Mann, 282–301. Urbana, IL: University of Illinois Press.
Beauvoir, Simone de. 2003. Pyrrhus et Cinéas. In *Pour une morale de l'ambiguïté suivi de Pyrrhus et Cinéas*, 199–316. Paris: Gallimard. English edition: Beauvoir, Simone de. 2004b. Pyrrhus and Cineas. In *Philosophical Writings*, eds Margaret A. Simons, Marybeth Timmermann and Mary Beth Mader, trans. Marybeth Timmermann, 89–149. Urbana, IL: University of Illinois Press.
Berliner, Wendy and Deborah Eyre. 2018. *Great Minds and How to Grow Them: High Performance Learning*. Abingdon, Oxon: Routledge.
Castner, Catherine J. 1982. Epicurean Hetairai as Dedicants to Healing Deities? *Greek, Roman and Byzantine Studies* 23 (1): 51–57.
Diogenes Laertius. 1972. *Lives of Eminent Philosophers,* Loeb Classical Library, ed. Robert Drew Hicks. Trans. Robert Hicks. Cambridge: Harvard University Press. http://www.perseus.tufts.edu/hopper/text?doc=D.%20L. Accessed 22 April 2022.

Dotson, Kristie. 2012. How Is This Paper Philosophy? *Comparative Philosophy* 3 (1): 3–29. http://scholarworks.sjsu.edu/cgi/viewcontent.cgi?article=1039&context=comparativephilosophy. Accessed 22 April 2022.
Extending New Narratives in the History of Philsophy. https://www.newnarrativesinphilosophy.net/index.html. Accessed 21 April 2022.
Fant, Maureen B. and Mary R. Lefkowitz. 1982. *Women's Life in Greece and Rome*. London: Duckworth.
Haslanger, Sally Anne. 2008. Changing the Ideology and Culture of Philosophy: Not by Reason (Alone). *Hypatia* 23 (2): 210–223.
Hannan, Barbara. 2009. *The Riddle of the World: A Reconsideration of Schopenhauer's Philosophy*. Oxford, NY: Oxford University Press.
Hedenborg, Susanna. 2007. Female Jockeys in Swedish Horse-Racing 1890–2000: From Minority to Majority—Complex Causes. *The International Journal of the History of Sport* 24 (4): 501–519.
Iser, Wolfgang. 1980. *The Act of Reading*. Baltimore, MD: John Hopkins University Press.
Kant, Immanuel. 2007. *Critique of Judgement*, ed. Nicholas Walker. Trans. James Creed Meredith. Oxford, NY: Oxford University Press.
Korhonen, Tua and Erika Ruonakoski. 2017. *Human and Animal in Ancient Greece: Empathy and Encounter in Classical Literature*. Library of Classical Studies. London: I.B.Tauris.
Lagier, Rosine. 2009. *La femme et le cheval: Des siècles d'histoire*. Janzé: Editions Charles Hérissey.
Le Dœuff, Michèle. 1989. The Philosophical Imaginary. Athlone: London
Lehtinen, Virpi. 2007. On Philosophical Style. *European Journal of Women's Studies* 14 (2): 109–125.
Margulis, Lynn. 2004. On Syphilis and the Nature of Nietzsche's Madness. *Dædalus* 133 (4), 118–125.
Merleau-Ponty, Maurice. 1998. *Phénoménologie de la perception*. Paris: Gallimard. English edition: Merleau-Ponty, Maurice. 2012. *Phenomenology of Perception*. Trans. Donald A. Landes. Abingdon: Routledge.
Meyer, Ursula I. 1997. *Philosophinnen-Lexikon*. Aachen: Ein-Fach-Verl.
Murray, Penelope. 1989. Introduction. *Genius: The History of an Idea*, ed. Penelope Murray, 1–6. Oxford, UK: Basil Blackwell.
Niederhoff, Burkhard. 2011a. Focalization. In *The Living Handbook of Narratology*, eds Peter Hühn et al. Hamburg: Hamburg University.
Niederhoff, Burkhard. 2011b. Perspective—Point of View. In *The Living Handbook of Narratology*, eds Peter Hühn et al. Hamburg: Hamburg University.
Oxenhandler, Neal. 1994. The Bodily Experience of Simone Weil. *L'Esprit Créateur*, 34 (3), 82–91.
Paxton, Molly, Carrie Figdor and Valerie Tiberius. 2012. Quantifying the Gender Gap: An Empirical Study of the Underrepresentation of Women in Philosophy. *Hypatia* 27 (4) 949–957.
Peters, Michael A. 2019. Wittgenstein and the Ethics of Suicide. Homosexuality and Jewish Self-Hatred in Fin de Siècle Vienna. *Educational Philosophy and Theory*, 51 (10), 981–990. https://doi.org/10.1080/00131857.2018.1548881.
Plant, Ian Michael. 2004. *Women Writers of Ancient Greece and Rome: An Anthology*. Norman: Oklahoma University Press.
Plato. 1998. *Republic*. Trans. Robin Waterfield. Oxford, NY: Oxford University Press.
Pletsch, Carl. 1991. *Young Nietzsche: Becoming a Genius*. New York, NY: Free Press.
Project Vox. http://projectvox.org/. Accessed 21 April 2022.
Querelle. http://querelle.ca/. Accessed 21 April 2022.
Rullmann, Marit. 1998a. *Philosophinnen, Band 1: Von Der Antike Bis Zur Aufklärung*. Frankfurt: Suhrkamp.
Rullmann, Marit. 1998b. *Philosophinnen, Band 2: Von Der Romantik Bis Zur Moderne*. Frankfurt: Suhrkamp.
Sadler, Brook J. 2004. How Important Is Student Participation in Teaching Philosophy? *Teaching Philosophy* 27 (3): 251–267.

Schmid, Wolf. 2013. Implied Author. In *The Living Handbook of Narratology*, eds Peter Hühn et al. Hamburg: Hamburg University.

Schopenhauer, Arthur. 1907. *On the Fourfold Root of the Principle of Sufficient Reason and on the Will in Nature: Two Essays.* Trans. Karl Hillebrand. London: Chiswick.

Tougas, Cecile T. and Sara Ebenreck. 2000. *Presenting Women Philosophers.* The New Academy. Philadelphia: Temple University Press.

Verene, Donald. 2018. The Genuine and Surrogate Canon: A Philosophical Education. *Sofia Philosophical Review* 11(1): 5–18.

Mary Ellen Waithe (ed.). 1987. *A History of Women Philosophers, Vol. 1: Ancient Women Philosophers 600 B.C.–A.D. 500*. Dordrecht: Martinus Nijhoff Publishers.

Mary Ellen Waithe (ed.). 1989. *A History of Women Philosophers, Vol. 2: Medieval, Renessaince and Enlightenment Women Philosophers A.D. 500–1600*. Dordrecht: Kluwer.

Mary Ellen Waithe (ed.). 1991. *A History of Women Philosophers, Vol. 3: Modern Women Philosophers A.D. 1600–1900*. Dordrecht: Kluwer

Mary Ellen Waithe (ed.). 1995. *A History of Women Philosophers, Vol. 4: Contemporary Women Philosophers: 1900–Today*. Dordrecht: Kluwer

White, Gina. 2003. Equine Sports: A Partnership in Fitness. *American Fitness* 21 (2): 22–24.

Wider, Kathleen. 1986. Women Philosophers in the Ancient Greek World: Donning the Mantle. *Hypatia* 1 (1): 21–62.

Open Access This chapter is licensed under the terms of the Creative Commons Attribution 4.0 International License (http://creativecommons.org/licenses/by/4.0/), which permits use, sharing, adaptation, distribution and reproduction in any medium or format, as long as you give appropriate credit to the original author(s) and the source, provide a link to the Creative Commons license and indicate if changes were made.

The images or other third party material in this chapter are included in the chapter's Creative Commons license, unless indicated otherwise in a credit line to the material. If material is not included in the chapter's Creative Commons license and your intended use is not permitted by statutory regulation or exceeds the permitted use, you will need to obtain permission directly from the copyright holder.

Chapter 4
The Affective, Social and Bodily Situation

Abstract This chapter deals with the affective, social and bodily situation of learning and teaching philosophy, starting with a discussion of the views articulated by both students and professional philosophers in the interviews and answers to the questionnaire on attitudes to studying philosophy. The discussions of women students' "love" or "passion" for philosophy and of the dynamics of alienation from philosophy lead to an examination of the alienation related to students' social class, race and sexual orientation. As we saw earlier, feminist pedagogy has typically tried to surpass the idea of reason that operates as separate from the feeling, sensing and moving body. In this chapter, I discuss the aspect of the senses and how they are and could be integrated in processes of learning more comprehensively. At the end of the chapter, I describe two summer schools. The first of these is the Icelandic one, Philosophy of the Body, which examined the possibility of teaching philosophy "through the body". The second is the Danish summer school titled Feminist Political Philosophy.

4.1 Women Students' Passion for and Alienation from Philosophy

How do women students and graduates experience the educational, collegial and institutional practices of philosophy? This section elucidates that experience on the basis of the background study conducted for the purposes of this book. To be sure, some of the concerns raised by women are also concerns of those who identify themselves as men or as belonging to a gender minority, and I return to this issue in the next section. For now, however, I focus on how women themselves interpret their feelings of belonging and not-belonging in the community of philosophers. Space is given to a plurality of views in the hope that together they help us draw some tentative conclusions of women's experiences of alienation.

To start from the positive aspects related to philosophy by all genders, these include the idea of philosophy as a field of intellectual freedom. As we remember, Aristotle suggests that philosophic wisdom offers "pleasures marvellous for their purity and their enduringness"; for him, philosophical contemplation is the only activity that "would seem to be loved for its own sake; for nothing arises from it apart from the contemplating, while from practical activities we gain more or less apart from the action" (*NE*; Aristotle 2001, X:7).

Not all philosophers entirely agree with Aristotle's view: from Plato to Wollstonecraft and from Marx to Arendt and Franz Fanon, many philosophers see philosophy as a force for social transformation. Even so, it may not be misguided to claim that the core of the philosophical attitude consists of intellectual curiosity, the attitude of wonder and constant search (see Heinämaa 2000). The aim is a better understanding of things, pursued in a community of thinkers who share the ideals of intellectual humility and bravery. It is this particular kind of camaraderie that philosophy majors are supposed to enjoy so much that they are ready to make it the centrepiece of their lives. To be sure, at its best philosophical activity brings about a shared intellectual joy and a sense of belonging.

Yet there are considerable differences in how students experience their philosophical education. Some of these differences became explicit in the background research conducted for this book. This study consisted of a small survey about students' attitudes to philosophy and a dozen interviews, most of them with philosophy majors, some with minors, and two with people who had a degree in philosophy but had left the field.[1] In the semi-structured interviews, interviewees could speak rather freely on the given theme, which here was their relationship to philosophy in general and the way they viewed gender in the context of philosophy. The interviewees and questionnaire respondents were from various countries (from Europe to the Americas and Asia), but due to my own affiliation with a Finnish university, Finns became the biggest group. Women formed the majority of the forty respondents and twelve interviewees. The goal was not to create a comprehensive empirical study of students' attitudes but rather to listen to the diverse experiences related to studying philosophy in view of the goals of this volume. This limitation must be taken into account when the material from the survey and interviews is interpreted.

Perhaps expectedly, especially philosophy majors found studying philosophy rewarding, while some who had taken only a few courses in philosophy after upper secondary school even showed hostile attitudes. When the respondents and interviewees were asked about the things they enjoy most in philosophy, many of them mentioned its breadth, depth and intellectual rigour. A woman philosophy major gave the following list of enjoyable things in philosophy:

> The issues discussed, the stringent mode of thinking and the dedication to really go to the bottom of things. The clarity of writing and use of words. The dedication to really be on point. The curiosity to really dig deep into fundamental questions. Philosophy has made me

---

[1] In the survey, most of the questions were open-ended, for instance: "What is it about philosophy that you like?" "What is it about philosophy that you do not like?" "Which, if any, are your favourite questions or themes in philosophy?" "Does a student's gender play any role in studying philosophy, in a negative or positive manner? In which ways?" Among the multiple-choice questions the most interesting one dealt with the feelings inspired by philosophy. Almost all the respondents named joy as a feeling inspired by philosophy. The other alternatives were success, absorption, enthusiasm, control, irritation, failure and inadequacy.

see everyday things with new eyes. The tools you get to analyse, question and understand parts of the world.

Another woman respondent described her interest in philosophy in a similar way:

I like that it takes nothing for granted, and that no question is unaskable. One can keep being surprised and keep going on to delve deeper into a subject. So, the radical critical attitude, in the sense that philosophy wants to understand the roots of everything, is what interests me the most.

It was not rare that philosophy majors expressed what could be called a passionate relationship to philosophy. Many students felt that philosophy had radically changed their ways of seeing the world; it had changed their lives. Their praises of philosophy were not unreserved, however. One of my interviewees, Laura,[2] pointed out that she was first impressed by the fact that all parts of reality were potential topics of philosophical reflection. She also felt that philosophy did, indeed, give her tools for thinking, and helped her to satisfy her intellectual curiosity. This aspect of philosophy was rewarding for her. At the same time, she had great expectations for the interaction between philosophy students, anticipating discussions that would be conducted in a tolerant atmosphere and would be broad in content. Nevertheless, she felt that these expectations were not met. She found that especially in the beginning of her studies, the atmosphere in the discussions between students was competitive and even aggressive. Open dialogue was difficult, because, according to her, some male students had "a downright religious attitude" towards theory: they idealised a chosen theory and clung to it instead of engaging freely in a dialogue.

Here we return to the problem framed by Le Dœuff: the ownership of knowledge. It is certainly typical of philosophy that its practitioners find security and shelter in a tradition of thought they choose to represent. Even if you may not be able to provide your own ideas about specific philosophical questions, you can always refer to the solutions of earlier philosophers. It can be useful to try out how a problem would be approached through a particular philosophical framework, even if you did not subscribe to it. This allows us to see if that framework could be fruitful in elaborating the question we are interested in. It can also be argued that a studious emulation of a philosophical framework is a necessary step on the way to freer thinking. The peril of this approach is that your thinking may become engulfed by a conceptual framework to such an extent that you cannot really conceive of alternative modes of thought, or that your interpretation of reality dogmatically follows your chosen theory or the ideas of a specific thinker. I will not take a stance on how gendered such a tendency is; yet it is clear that a dedication to a theory allows you to present yourself as a possessor of knowledge, that is, living in the wealth of knowledge instead of moving between wealth and poverty, as Eros described by Diotima in Plato's *Symposium*.[3]

Yet the apparently self-purposeful accumulation of knowledge about a specific theory or approach can be an answer to the feelings of inadequacy philosophy majors

---

[2] The names of the interviewees have been changed.

[3] About love and wonder as attitudes of philosophising and an analysis of *The Symposium*, see Heinämaa (2000, 2017).

may have in the beginning of their studies. The very same things that make philosophy so alluring, namely its breadth of history and topics, its depth and open-endedness, also make it very challenging to get a grasp of. Facing this challenge, students may overestimate the demands of the discipline, and underestimate their own abilities. One of the women respondents explained how her love for philosophy was overshadowed by feelings of inadequacy:

> I love this subject and I have felt a strong feeling of privilege and happiness about being able to study this subject. But I also got depressed when writing my bachelor's thesis because (among other things) of not feeling good enough. I thought I would not manage to write the thesis, but then I got an A. It felt like a joke afterwards that I had gone through so much anguish about something that, as it turned out, I was really good at.

While these unwarranted feelings of inadequacy are not entirely gender-specific, several studies that do not specifically focus on philosophy show that it is more typical for male students (at school and university) to overestimate their performance and more typical for female students to underestimate theirs. It is also typical for male students to underestimate the performance of their female peers. (E.g. Bench et al. 2015; Cole et al. 1999; Grunspan et al. 2016). All in all, it seems that even if girls, as a group, tend to do better in upper secondary school (or high school) than boys, a significant proportion of women philosophy students are not ready to take up speaking space with the same confidence as men, nor do they trust their abilities in philosophy. What came up repeatedly in the interviews and questionnaires was that the image of the philosopher was quite gendered. The above-quoted woman student, who has a passionate relationship to philosophy, describes her alienation from it as follows:

> I do not feel that I have been discriminated against. I feel, though, that being in a male majority context has at times made me more insecure. I also feel that I have a picture of the ideal philosopher being male, and that I have had a hard time seeing myself as a person who can do the sorts of things that philosophers do, and answer those types of questions they do.

On the surface, it seems that adopting an identity as a professional philosopher may come more easily to men than women. Some female students also feel that they get less attention and recognition than male students or that they have to work harder to be recognised by the faculty and their peers. Some also suggest that assertiveness and confrontation—attitudes more often linked with the traditional masculine virtues than the feminine ones—are overly appreciated in the philosophy class:

> I think it is very easy for a philosophy class to turn into an environment that rewards rhetorical confidence and assertiveness over substance. Confrontation is sometimes overly rewarded as well. I think that the norms of femininity tend to clash with this environment and make women think "this is not for me". But, even when women don't think that, the problem is that men think it is "for them". That is to say, I have seen too many young men who seem to think they are naturally gifted in philosophy, with very little evidence. Their self-image seems to adhere to the discipline very easily. And this leads them to be very controlling in discussions, take up too much space and be often condescending towards women students. I feel the kind of young men who are in this category are (coincidentally or not) those most likely to not to treat their fellow women students as colleagues and not to be critical of current gendered norms and arrangements.

In contrast to this woman student's personal dissatisfaction with the behaviour of some men students, for most men students whom I interviewed or who answered to the questionnaire, the realisation that gender bias was possible always came through the complaints of women students. In other words, practices that generate inequality had remained hidden to them until women students had addressed the issue. As in the case of race, privilege is difficult to discern from the perspective of the privileged.

There may also be cultural and institutional differences in whether confrontational strategies are rewarded or not. Even within a specific institution the work culture evolves over time, depending, among other things, on the changes in the staff. Unfortunately, it may take only one person with a condescending attitude to cause a lot of resentment, especially if no one protests against the person's derogatory comments.

However, the complaints of women philosophy majors are mild in comparison to those of women in other fields. It is my impression—and further research would be needed to validate this—that many women from the outgroup find philosophers' way of interacting complacent and the discipline itself dry. In these cases, philosophers are seen as arrogant and uninterested in what really goes on in the world, indifferent to empirical evidence and unwilling to pay attention to the changes and new challenges in the society. Fields outside philosophy appear to these women as more appealing, more exciting, more up-to-date, and most importantly, less permeated by smugness and self-assertion.

Especially women with a background in gender studies voice these kinds of criticisms of philosophy, even though many of them also have a profound interest in the discipline.[4] Emma, a gender studies major, pointed out that she found the teaching of the philosophy classes she had taken old-fashioned and violent in the sense that they reproduced old stereotypes about gender. According to another student of gender studies, philosophy encourages one to disdain the thoughts of others (non-philosophers) and involves a futile splitting of hairs. Yet others suggested that professional philosophers complicate philosophical discussion in order to be able to monopolise it, to keep non-professionals at bay.

Of course, one way to respond to such criticism—if it ever reaches the ears of philosophers—is to attribute it to the ignorance of laypersons. Even so, this criticism is parallel to those that all genders *within* the field engage in, as we will see in the next section. As for women's experienced distance from the field, this may have to do with the homosocial situation in which its norms are created, as I suggested earlier.

No matter how benevolent the male staff is towards female students, the dynamics between heterosexual male staff and students can be effortless in a way that is difficult to achieve with female students. For instance, the framework of one-on-one discussions with staff members can be quite different for male and female students. In her post on the *Women in Philosophy* website, a female graduate student points out the difference between her own attitude towards the possibility of sexual harassment and that of her boyfriend's, who was also a graduate student in philosophy. Unlike the

---

[4] In the background study, after the philosophy majors and professionals, the second biggest group were women students in gender studies. This may be why the latter stand out as the critical ones.

boyfriend, she was always painfully aware of the possibility of sexual underpinnings and misunderstandings in one-on-one meetings:

> whenever I have ever had a meeting with a male member of staff I am on some level worried that they might express interest in me, or that I will realise that they are interested in me, or that they will think that I am interested in them.[5]

This example shows how heteronormativity plays out at least for some women in a male-dominated setting. The necessity to make sure that the situation is not understood as sexually charged can make the relationship more awkward than it might be otherwise. Naturally the situation is even worse, if the student is treated primarily as a sexual object, which means that her value as a prospective colleague is diminished.

Similar situations may occur when the roles are reversed: hooks describes an incident between herself and a male student to whom she, without totally acknowledging it, had become attracted. In order to outweigh her erotic feelings, she treated the young man so dismissively that he finally complained about her behaviour (hooks 1994, 192).[6] Given that philosophy faculty is predominantly male, it could be assumed that female students have more limited space than male students in their interactions with the staff.

In a small Finnish survey, a female respondent compares the situations of male and female students in the following manner:

> In the beginning of my studies I noticed that male students also spent more of their free time with the department staff. I myself did not feel I knew anyone on the department staff, nor did I believe any of them would remember my name. I remember a discussion I had when I was writing my master's thesis. [One of the male students] stated that since his freshman year, he had spent time mainly with the faculty. Young men do not appear to question their knowledge and abilities so much. At the same time, young women communicate continuous uncertainty about their competence and skills. In my class the young, clearly talented women, who also did well in their studies, did not feel capable of becoming philosophers or doing philosophical research. I'm the only one in that group who continued in philosophy after the master's thesis[7] (Halttunen-Riikonen 2014, 108).

Even if the close relationship to the faculty described by the male student were not all that common, this quotation sheds light on the sense of being adrift shared by many women students. The distance experienced by the woman respondent from the faculty did not prevent her from continuing to doctoral studies, but, in her interpretation, such was not the case with her female peers.

Even after entering the doctoral or postdoctoral phase, an individual can still experience the hierarchical structures of the department as alienating. One of my interviewees, Anna, who had left academic philosophy some years after obtaining her doctorate, found the hierarchical life at the philosophy department troubling, as it was in such a stark contrast to the what she considered to be the spirit of philosophy

---

[5] https://beingawomaninphilosophy.wordpress.com/category/relationships-with-students/. Accessed 1 April 2022.

[6] hooks's examples are not from a philosophy class, as she herself taught English and Ethnic Studies.

[7] My translation.

4.1 Women Students' Passion for and Alienation from Philosophy

itself. Emphasising that zeal for climbing the career ladder is not necessarily more typical of men than women, Anna suggested that women might be less interested in philosophy as an institution, and that many of them feel that there is a tension between philosophy as dialogue and as institution.

> [A]dvancing in philosophy requires a specific integrity and independence, a critical use of reason […] but I don't see that it wouldn't be equally possible for both women and men. Wanting to learn and wanting to conquer new areas of knowledge, a critical use of reason, and a courage to express this… this is a combination that can be found in both genders, but women […] have less to lose.

Anna suggests that due to their historical situation outside or in the margins of academic philosophy, it may be easier for women to extend their philosophical wonder to the life of the institution itself. As she sees it, most male students are more inclined to experience the practice of philosophy as a unified, valuable whole, including its institutional aspects:

> It is more important for men to be included in the institution. [The institution] is, in a way, a different thing than a community. When I think about the community of women [philosophers], I don't think about their positions in academia or about their career paths. But young men are very much aware of career paths. This is the difference. Women do philosophy for its content or in the framework of the intellectual community, […] and men see its formal aspect, and are interested in it, because it is built by their forefathers. There is something more interesting in it for them. This was, again, exactly what pushed me away from it […]. There are, of course, […] many good sides to the institutionalisation as well […], but the institution [of philosophy] wouldn't have to be quite like it is now […]. It could be determined more by content and the community, and less by the structures. I find that this formal showing off may push women away, also other women than myself. It's uninteresting.

From Anna's perspective, the institutional aspect of philosophy should be questioned and rebuilt in such a way that the practice of thinking together comes first: philosophy is worthwhile in its connection to everyday life, or when the ethical, the practical and the theoretical form a seamless whole.

As we have seen, women's alienation from philosophy may have to do with how people respond to them. One of my interviewees, Lea, described her transition as a loss of privilege within the philosophical arena. When she had returned to her studies after a break, having entered the transition, she felt that her speaking space was no longer respected as it had been when she had occupied a man's role. Other students would talk out of turn and interrupt her in seminars, and even her physical space seemed reduced. People would no longer step aside to let her pass, and in public spaces, they would come much closer to her than used to be the case. Yet she had not shrunk physically, and refused to live her body in the inhibited manner that now appeared to be required of her:

> I express myself very aggressively and clearly, I don't watch my mouth or move cautiously, […] and the lecturers don't quite know how to react to that, how to respond. […] But what is the boundary that I transgress here? Is the problem that I am a trans person or do they wonder why this woman is like this? Why do I jump over desks as a woman? But this is the way that I am accustomed to act and move, I'm not cautious about my environment […] and I don't want to be because it would be dishonest towards myself, and I would concretely have to hide myself.

All in all, she felt that she had lost "the protective field of masculinity" that she once had. Being used to this protection and to being heard, she found the vanishing of her privilege disconcerting. Lea's experience would then appear to confirm what is suspected by students who are cis women, namely that their gender makes their arguments less interesting.

To summarise, women's alienation from philosophy appears to include, at least, the following aspects: (1) feeling of distance from the faculty, (2) the occasional gender-based role of underdog in classroom confrontations, (3) difficulties to identify oneself with the traditional masculine role of the philosopher, (4) the dominance of the all-knowing attitude over not-knowing, (5) underestimation of one's abilities by oneself and others, (6) difficulty in acquiring speaking space and (7) frustration with academic philosophy as an institution. Instead of attributing all these aspects to the experiences of all women in philosophy, I would suggest that they form a pattern that is familiar in differing aspects to different women. All things considered, however, it would seem that many women students may need support from the teaching staff to be able to live up to their potential. Before examining potential ways to provide this support, I demonstrate how the problem of alienation extends far beyond the situation of women students.

4.2 Class, Race and Sexual Orientation

"Philosophy is not for black women. That is a white man's game". This is advice a career counsellor gave to the US philosopher Kristie Dotson's younger sister, who had suggested that she too might want to become a professional philosopher. British philosopher Patricia Haynes, who has a Caribbean background, recalled her father's reaction to her idea of making a career out of philosophy: "Philosophy is for posh white boys with trust funds" (Ratcliffe and Shaw 2015). At the moment of writing the article, Haynes identified herself as one of the three Black women philosophers in Great Britain. According to Charles W. Mills, the US-based author of *Blackness Visible: Essays on Philosophy and Race*, there are "so few recognized black philosophers that the term still has something of an oxymoronic ring to it" (1998, 2).

In these examples three characteristics are attributed to philosophy: Whiteness, maleness and affluence. Yet the class status of studying philosophy varies from one country to another. In the Nordic countries, where university education does not— as of yet—require a financial input from the parents, studying philosophy is not generally associated with a high socioeconomic status. In some other countries, such a status may be taken for granted among students, as a woman student describes:

> Philosophy has a gender problem. But, at least in North America, it also seems to have a very big race and class problem. One very obvious way in which this manifests itself is the plain underrepresentation of students from diverse backgrounds in graduate programmes. It leads to the formation of a certain social "consensus", of an imagined shared background that is distinctively affluent and "white" American. For example, I have felt quite alienated

4.2 Class, Race and Sexual Orientation

from many informal social occasions among philosophers because of the level of wealth and the economic family background assumed in conversation. The gap is so big that I feel like I cannot relate to those people and I often withdraw from conversation altogether. This carries over to philosophical discussions where I am sometimes shocked by the lack of familiarity with other more disadvantaged economic situations (and also the explicit assumption that everyone in the room is unfamiliar with them).

It has been suggested that students from the Nordic countries also participate in an academic culture based on the lifestyle and values of the middle and upper classes. Sociological studies have shown that women students and researchers that come from a working-class background, may feel continuing insecurity within academia, not having immersed the middle- and upper-class values that produce the ability to discuss and analyse even minor issues at length, to speak out, take space and present arguments with self-confidence (e.g. Käyhkö 2014, 10–12) (Ibid., 13–14.). In their homes, they may have had to differentiate from values that present manual labour as more worthwhile and honest than academic work, which is "just studying" or even "wasting tax-payers' money". Despite their possible success in academia, many working-class students and researchers experience a constant need to prove themselves, a fear "being found out" as lacking, and a feeling of discomfort.

In his answer to the questionnaire about studying philosophy, a male student describes the impact of his working-class background as follows:

I come from a lower working-class background in which I was the first in my entire family to even graduate from high school.[8] I do not come from a literary home. This means a lack of cultural background that is beneficial to studying a topic like philosophy and a great and persistent feeling of insecurity, inadequacy and being an "imposter" who is out of his element.

Despite the fact that he is able to articulate his thoughts in an eloquent manner, he still feels like "an imposter" and "out of his element" in philosophy.[9] This feeling of incongruence or alienation is parallel to that of students with ties to a non-majority culture, women students, students of colour, and students with disabilities. At the same time these experiences of alienation and incongruence are not present in a uniform manner within or across these divisions: a White female student with an academic family background may feel more at ease in classroom debates than a White male student with a working-class background, whereas she may experience more feelings of discomfort in in some other parts of the student life, like male-dominated informal get-togethers. In other words, the experiences of alienation and incongruence have a somewhat fluctuating character: often they are born from exclusions from the White, Western, cis male, middle-class, heterosexual, able-bodied norm, but at

---

[8] In the Nordic countries, the compulsory education lasts for nine years and consists of a primary school of six years and a middle school of three years, the latter equivalent to the lower grades of the American high school. After that one spends three more years in upper secondary education, either in a vocational or an academic school. The latter, again, is equivalent to the higher grades of the American high school. So, when the respondent says that he was the first in his family to graduate from high school, he means that he was the first to go through an academic upper secondary school that prepares its students for university studies.

[9] About the "imposter syndrome", see Sandra Lee Bartky (2003).

other times these exclusions are less apparent and can be compensated by privileges or "strengths" in other areas (upbringing in an academic home, cultural know-how, good self-confidence).

In "How Is This Paper Philosophy?" (2012), Dotson identifies within philosophy "a culture of justification" that prevents minority philosophers from feeling at ease within the field. By "culture of justification" she means a system which requires that all scholars justify their methods, topics and pedagogical choices with a "traditional" conception of philosophical engagement (Dotson 2012, 6). Analysing more specifically the situation of philosophers of colour, Dotson draws from the work of Gayle Salamon, according to whom justification as a method requires congruence and reconciliation of differences and is therefore particularly ill-suited to queer theory: "queerness as a method would proceed in the opposite way, by supposing a diversion or estrangement from the norm and using that divergence as a source of proliferation and multiplication with the aim of increasing the livability of those lives outside of the norm" (Salamon 2009, 229).[10]

Dotson suggests that to make philosophy more inclusive, philosophers should work towards a disciplinary culture where "incongruence becomes a site of creativity for ever-expanding ways of doing professional philosophy" and multiple canons are accepted as a point of departure for philosophy (2012, 16–17). She also argues that the view of philosophy as a fundamentally critical enterprise and the necessity to adjust to a fairly restricted set of questions may alienate minority practitioners from philosophy (ibid., 20–21).

Mills in turn sees the false universalism of mainstream philosophy as an important reason for the underrepresentation of Black people in the discipline. In his view, it is the theoretical or conceptual Whiteness of the discipline itself rather than the skin colour of philosophers that makes philosophy alienating for Black students. (Mills 1998, 2). He underlines that in the history of Western philosophy the situation of Black people, who are hardly ever mentioned, differs from that of women, who are continuously disparaged. The history of Black slavery and subordination do not figure in the abstractions and ideals formulated by White philosophers. From the viewpoint of Black students, a lot of moral philosophy seems to be "based on pretense, the claim that these were the principles that people strove to uphold, when in fact the real principles were the racially exclusivist ones" (Mills 1998, 4).

From this perspective, it does not seem that the basic reason for the underrepresentation of minority students in philosophy would be related to explicit discrimination. Yet discrimination does exist: in Finland, for instance, many secondary school students with an immigrant background feel pressured by guidance counsellors to

---

[10] One could, perhaps, say that feminist philosophy in general, too, sees divergence as a resource and richness, not as something that needs justification. The goals of White feminists, however, have been criticised by Black feminists. In *Feminism is for Everybody* (hooks 2000), hooks argues that in the 1970s, White feminists wanted to "own" feminism and refused to see that their issues were not the most relevant ones for Black women. For instance, White feminists wanted to be included in the same work market of the men of their class, whereas Black women in low-paying jobs already were, and did not find their liberation in it. According to hooks, then, feminism as such is not necessarily inclusive or welcoming towards the diverse concerns of different minorities.

4.2 Class, Race and Sexual Orientation

get a practical rather than a theoretical education (Airas et al. 2019, 68). Role models and family support help such students to see different career paths as possible for themselves (ibid., 75), but if we are to take Mills's words seriously, we will see that philosophy can seem insignificant from the viewpoint of minorities, not only because it is not a financially secure career option but because it ignores their history, experience and very existence.

Mills likewise argues that due to their racially privileged position, White students tend to interpret their own experiences as *human* rather than racial. This is why they understand also their relationship to the world as *the* relationship to the world rather than as one of racial privilege (Mills 1998, 10).

According to Mills, making White philosophy students aware of Black experience may require integrating elements from sociology and history in the teaching. Consequently, the philosophy class may seem "less like philosophy" from the viewpoint of White students, and they start to think of African-American philosophy as something that deviates from actual philosophy (See Mills 1998, 10). Raising awareness of the history of women or feminist approaches in philosophy classes may meet with similar resistance.

When the discipline of philosophy shows that it not only tolerates but appreciates the study of politically charged areas and the experience of minorities, minority students will feel more drawn towards philosophy. Pedagogically this means integrating courses that deal with such charged issues, and hiring lecturers from diverse backgrounds. Most crucially, the importance of the point of view should be acknowledged: we should be able to understand that often philosophical discussions of ethics and humanity reflect only the experience of the privileged class, race and gender. This is the most difficult step to take, because it involves a change in how White philosophers themselves understand philosophy. In practice, this change would involve discussing questions such as slavery, the colonial heritage of Europe or the position of disabled people routinely in our classes. Increasing sensitivity about the plurality of human experience is challenging, however, for it requires us to abandon the illusion of ourselves as the possessors of the universal point of view.

In a similar vein as Dotson and Mills, Carlos Sanchez has pointed out that mainstream philosophy, which in his view holds disembodiment, ahistoricity and universality as its ideals, does not allow a discussion of questions of marginality, and judges philosophies that are able to address them as falsely profound.[11] For a "homegrown" US Hispanic philosopher, then, to adapt oneself to the mainstream would require "looking away" from everything that makes one Hispanic (Sanchez 2011, 40; see also Dotson 2012, 14, and hooks 1994, 192). In Chapter Three, I suggested that rootedness in philosophy requires either an intuitive connection to some of the generally discussed themes in the field or working out one's own history as an embodied and gendered practitioner of philosophy. Such a requirement can leave minority practitioners without a rooted existence within philosophy. They can go through the motions of academic philosophy, but this exercise can remain void of meaning if

---

[11] For a discussion of disembodiment and embodiment in philosophical writing, see e.g. Thorgeirsdottir (2020) and Lehtinen (2007).

they cannot orient towards new ideas with the support of their personal history and ethnic background.

The question of embodiment in philosophy is not necessarily limited to the research interests of philosophers who are women or belong to other minorities, but it can be that their very presence as "different" bodies stirs up the status quo and makes embodiment in general explicit. Anna suggests that in philosophy the body represents incoherence and chaos, and that "women represent corporeality in a different way than men".

Should it then be thought that the presence of, for instance, a woman or a homosexual man can at least at times interfere with the rules and routines of social interaction between heterosexual cis men and remind them of their own sexual and vulnerable bodies? Lea reflects upon the invisibility of homosexual men in the philosophical community in the following way:

> In philosophy, there appear to be very few people from sexual minorities. Either people are extremely good at being silent about it or there are [hardly any]. […] I believe it would be difficult for gay men to function within philosophy. I think that it is always easier for lesbian women than for gay men, because the more masculine a structure is, the more difficult it is precisely for gay men to come out. […] Perhaps it can be seen here that when a discipline is male-dominated, and supported by male relationships, the position of gay men can become difficult, because they can also unbalance… well, what could be called a safe relation between men.

It is, of course, difficult to assess the situation of gay men in philosophy without an empirical study, but it does seem that despite the presence of many prominent lesbian and bisexual women philosophers and gay philosophers such as Michel Foucault at the philosophical scene, and despite the origins of European philosophy in a more or less "bisexually" organised community of men,[12] heterosexuality has long been taken for granted as far as men philosophers are concerned. This may change, as the more liberal ways in which younger generations understand gender and sexuality become predominant.

Incidentally, it is in feminist and queer philosophy that embodiment and sexuality are considered as relevant or even central topics for philosophy. Questions of topics and methods are certainly intertwined with philosophy's problem of "disembodiment". While some students declared that their love for philosophy had to do with precision and abstraction, others complained about the exclusively abstract and game-like character of mainstream philosophy. When students were asked "what is it about philosophy that you do not like?", they most often pointed towards the overemphasis on reason and the alienation of philosophy from everyday life. This response, however, did not seem to be tied to the gender of respondents. For instance, one of the male students found it disturbing that "at times, [philosophy] can be very detached, academically self-centred and arrogant". This critique concerns the relationship to other disciplines: that philosophy fails to acknowledge what other disciplines have to offer. Another male student described his grievances as follows:

---

[12] To use words "homosexual", "bisexual" and "heterosexual" in the context of ancient Greece is, of course, anachronistic (see Foucault 1990).

I am less fond of philosophy as "puzzle solving". I used to like that but it is not really that interesting to me any more. I am thinking of the wide-spread practices of conceptual analysis and definitions, and of thinking of abstract hypothetical problems or scenarios that others then try to think of equally hypothetical counter-examples to. I am also not fond of the tendencies in philosophy that mostly seem to be about making up new words and to critique texts and concepts that relate to other texts which refer back to yet other texts but never seem to have any relevance in the world outside those texts. Both are examples of abstract and purely theoretical philosophy that doesn't actually try to understand the world but only creates a world of its own to play with.

In other words, the fact that students find philosophy to be alienated from the world produces at least in part their own alienation from philosophy. A woman student, in turn, points out that in philosophy "emotions are in the way (instead of being harnessed into energy for individuals and groups)".

In this section we have come to see that embodiment has political and social implications and that for many students, philosophy is burdened by a forgetfulness of the body. In what follows, the consideration of embodiment is broadened to the senses and how these can be engaged in learning situations.

4.3 Further Reflections on Embodiment

When understood in the phenomenological sense, the word "bodily" adds little to the expression "bodily situation". The body is then conceived as the body-subject that is both lived and materially present to itself and others. Consequently, all experienced situations are, in a way, bodily. All bodily situations are always permeated by social relationships and history, because we as body-subjects are social and historical beings. If we focus on the material–experiential reality of the body, however, we come to see how our bodies carry a lot of sedimented information that may not be directly available to our faculty of reasoning but is still sensed in specific situations.

If the COVID-19 pandemic has taught us anything, it is the significance of physical presence. It has made visible the importance of informal interaction before, during and after the class: when this is missing, in other words, when peer support is scarce, something very important seems to be lacking and learning acquires an indefinable heaviness. In online classes, some opt out from keeping their cameras on, and this makes it difficult for others to interpret their reactions. At the same time, it is challenging to be visually present to others and oneself through the camera and to process the information of the numerous faces on one's screen. In some online seminars, however, the experience of the presence of others can be even more forceful than in on-campus courses, and an intimate, trusting atmosphere can be created within the group. The situation is complex, because individuals tend to experience camera presence in different ways, and what is the sine qua non of good interaction for some is off-putting for others.

Nevertheless, other variables related to our experiences of embodiment may contribute to overcoming the difficulties of remote learning. As a personal experience, I can relate how, in an online seminar, discussing a text on body memory and bringing up personal examples of the working of body memory were as such enough to activate lived, bodily located and sedimented experiences in us. Then again, in another situation and with another group, when the same text was discussed merely theoretically, the same experiential depth and intimacy between group members was not reached.

In the first case, it was possible to reach the different layers of bodily existence even without any specific exercises of "the body". Yet, as I have suggested, there are other, more systematic ways of trying to surpass the one-dimensional way we tend to be present as bodies in academic learning and teaching. These involve a heightened interest in how we live our bodies and in the relevance of body position, movement, breathing or touch in the learning process. The challenge is to learn how to connect the philosophical content to a more multidimensional approach to embodiment. This connection is almost absent from such philosophical debates on embodiment and intersubjectivity in which the speakers shy from expressive body movements and fail to make eye contact with the audience, but also from experiments with movement or sound that take place merely for their own sake.

Yet another way to approach the question of embodiment in philosophy can be found in experiments that actually help the participants learn and analyse topics related to embodiment, such as perception, which they are studying. For instance, a "soundwalk" through chosen soundscapes can be taken with a facilitator, who has designed the route.[13] The idea of a soundwalk is to silently walk the designed route, focusing most of one's attention on what one hears in the environment, such as the sound of gravel underfoot, car tyres, seagulls, traffic lights. The inventors of soundwalk see it predominantly in terms of learning about the soundscape and participating in it, but it can also help us learn about the significance of focus in perception—how, with focus, what normally is experienced as "background noise" becomes a continuum of diverse and often intriguing sounds.

To be sure, lived experience is a more solid foundation for philosophical questioning than merely reading about the topic. It can also help students come up with ideas and questions that they address to the teaching staff, who in turn can use these as a basis for their teaching.

In assignments involving the senses, students can be asked to describe variations of touching, for instance, in the light of Merleau-Ponty's phenomenology of the body. How do touching the surface of a table, a piece of velvet, water, one's own hand or a dog's paw differ from each other? Basically, learning about philosophies of perception and embodiment makes the integration of any number of sense-related

---

[13] For instructions, see Hildegard Westerkamp's webpages, https://www.hildegardwesterkamp.ca/sound/installations/Nada/soundwalk/. Accessed 21 April 2022. Westerkamp's way of describing sound and its relationship with the body draw from mysticism rather than phenomenological philosophy, which has been my perspective here, but the practical instructions provided on the website are useful, whichever perspective we adopt. I am indebted to Janne Vanhanen for introducing the concept of soundwalk to me.

4.3 Further Reflections on Embodiment

experiments possible. Students who already have some background in these fields can be asked to analyse different kinds of philosophical texts or academic practices from the viewpoint of embodiment.

It is evident that when choosing their methods of teaching and learning, lecturers are also choosing the kind of humanity they want to promote. The ancient schools of philosophy definitely also proposed ways of life to their students, and, as we saw for the Pythagoreans, practices related with mysticism. What remains for each of us to think through personally is this: is philosophy a way of life, and if so, should it openly involve other kinds of practices than seminar discussions and drinking parties, to help students develop as bodily subjects that are able to care for themselves and others? Or, is it rather the task of the lecturer to make students aware of the fact that while engaging in their intellectual activities, they are participating in a number of embodied practices that come to structure their everyday existence and that it is possible to either to accept them without questioning or to actively and reflectively participate in the recreation of such practices? How are these practices related to our experiences of being rooted in our lives and in philosophy?

In our summer schools, the questions of rootedness and embodiment were addressed in very different ways. The Jyväskylä Summer School attempted to bring about rootedness in philosophy through providing a history of women thinkers. The Aalborg Summer School gave a detailed method of practising philosophy, with the idea that the focus on the method rather than on the master–disciple relationship might emancipate the students. At the Oslo Summer School, again, the contextuality of ethical choices was emphasised in order to discuss the relationship between the subject of philosophy and the world in a non-reductionist manner. At the University of Iceland the very idea of philosophy as a purely reason-based practice was called into question, and a number of practices were introduced in order to create a new beginning for philosophising. The following section addresses the approach proposed by the Icelandic summer school.

4.4 The Reykjavík Summer School: Nature, Emotions and the Body

The experimental summer school on Philosophy of the Body, designed by Sigridur Thorgeirsdottir, was held at the University of Iceland in Reykjavík. Again, the majority of the thirty participants came from the Nordic Erasmus+ partnership universities, but there were also participants from other European and North American universities. In all, 83% of the participants were women, and 17% were men.

The goal of the summer school was to challenge current academic practices as still based on a dualist conception of subjectivity and thereby incorporate an alienation from the lived body. According to the organisers, these practices are blind to the body's intertwining with the natural world. In their article "Reclaiming Nature by Reclaiming the Body" Guðbjörg R. Jóhannesdóttir and Thorgeirsdottir argue that while the conception of nature as a place outside of us is limited, it is not a good alternative to abandon the concept of nature altogether as the so-called end-of-nature theorists have done. The place to start reconceptualising nature and its power to surprise us and to take hold of us is within ourselves, in our experience "of being nature ourselves, of being bodies, of connecting to the core of what it means to be a breathing, pulsating, sexuate human being", of the fact that "we *are* something before we start thinking and having ideas" (Jóhannesdóttir and Thorgeirsdottir 2016, 41). This extended notion of the gendered body was thematised from both the phenomenological and social constructivist perspectives in the Reykjavík Summer School.[14] The theoretical treatment of embodiment and gender formed a foundation for the more practical approach to embodied thinking introduced in the course.

In the end of their article, Jóhannesdóttir and Thorgeirsdottir sketch a way of thinking that goes beyond the traditional Western rationalising, detached mode of thought:

> we should try to think like water and sense like plants – sense closely and feel how we touch and shape and are shaped by the riverbank we are flowing in, and allow our thoughts to flow from our bodies rather than restricting them to what can be squeezed through the workings of the analytical mind (Jóhannesdóttir and Thorgeirsdottir 2016, 47).

The mode of thinking outlined here was explicitly expressed in the pedagogical point of departure chosen for the Icelandic summer school. That point of departure was *focusing* or thinking through the body, as developed by the philosopher–psychologist Eugen T. Gendlin.[15] His philosophy starts from the idea that a deep bodily awareness profoundly influences people's lives. He calls this awareness "a felt sense". Focusing consists of getting in touch with this felt sense: paying attention to what is obscurely experienced in the body, and by staying with the unclear

---

[14] For a social constructivist discussion of gender and embodiment, see Sveinsdóttir (2015) and Witt (2011).

[15] In another article, "The Torn Robe of Philosophy: Philosophy as a Woman in *The Consolation of Philosophy* by Boethius" (Thorgeirsdottir 2020), Thorgeirsdottir discusses similar views on the practice of philosophy by a much earlier thinker, Boethius.

felt sense, going through different steps that produce a change in one's body and in one's way of understanding things (Gendlin 2007, 37).

Thomas Fuchs has discussed the "felt sense" of focusing in the context of body memory, emphasising the aspect of the lived body as historical. According to Fuchs, approaches such as focusing can help those who engage in them to "open the meaning cores of body memory and untangle their latent motives and feelings" (Fuchs 2012, 20).

Focusing requires turning towards the embodied self. Still, it allows for dwelling on specific problems, themes, words and concepts, getting in touch with their felt sense, discovering their felt meaning. Another central component of focusing is active listening, which requires that the listener makes space for truly hearing the other, and waits with a sense of wonder for how the other wants to fill that space. The listener should not give advice, interpret, judge or argue. The person being listened to should share only what feels right, and not be afraid to correct the listener, if the listener has not understood. In active listening, the focus is on listening and on the person being listened to, not on the listener (Gendlin 1996).

The course incorporated several practices of active listening. In one exercise students formed groups of three. One person spoke about their way of experiencing the lecture just given. Another was the listener, who focused on completely on the speaker, silently listening to them. Finally, the third person took notes about the speaker's account. When the speaker had ended their story, the notetaker read those notes aloud the them, and the speaker could comment on the notes, perhaps adding something or further specifying what was meant.

Together with Mary Hendricks, Gendlin also developed a novel method for philosophical thinking, "thinking at the edge" (2004). At the Icelandic summer school, the students were first familiarised with the basics of focusing, after which they were given practical "thinking at the edge" assignments by one of the lecturers, Donata Schoeller. "The edge" means a space in thinking in which one approaches the felt sense of the problem. Hesitation, faltering and struggling for words are interpreted as signs of entering the space of felt meaning. In one exercise, the lecturer facilitated the students' thinking process. While a student uses a method of association to rearticulate the central ideas of their project by replacing some of the key words by alternative ones, the facilitator listens, takes notes, and reflects back those parts in the student's speech that seem particularly meaningful, or "glowing", paying attention to the bodily, affective expressions of the student in reference to what they are discussing. The aim of this process is to facilitate a positive shift in the student's thinking in a way that does not shut out the embodied nature of human existence but embraces it as a resource for thinking (Gendlin 2017).

All in all, the course organisers wanted to experiment in and make room for experiential thinking, embodiment and emotions in philosophy. The lectures dealt with different philosophies of the body, bringing Gendlin's philosophy of the implicit, phenomenology of the body and social constructivism into contact with each other. As for spatial arrangements, the lectures took place in conventional classrooms, but for the group exercises students could freely use the different spaces in the university building. As a nature excursion was a part of the programme, Icelandic nature with its mountains and hot springs was one of the learning spaces. The syllabus was quite varied, integrating lectures, panels, different kinds of exercises and feedback sessions, and ending with a theme-based research question seminar.

During the summer school, we noticed that introducing experimental practices such as focusing and thinking at the edge requires a lot of advance planning and preparation. It is pivotal to make sure that, from the first, all the participants are aware of what kind of learning process and content they are engaging with, for students of philosophy tend to have fairly fixed sets of expectations towards what a philosophy class should be like. The learning experiments of the Reykjavík Summer School required adopting a quite different attitude from the typical critical and argumentative stance of the philosophy student, namely one that incorporates openness and trustfulness. Students who are drawn towards exploring embodiment through diverse practices and are looking for a relief from what they see as the overly rationalist atmosphere in philosophy certainly find it easier to immerse themselves in the exercises than students who are not oriented in this way. Bringing focusing methods into the classroom requires a highly competent facilitator, not least because of the emotional component of the exercises.

In a meaningful way, this summer school demonstrated the lack of attentive listening in academic life: while academia purports to embrace dialogue, even in seminars one very often focuses more on one's next argument than on what the other is saying. Even if one does not engage in actual "active listening" or "thinking at the edge" exercises with students, it can be helpful for teaching staff to go through these or similar exercises to be able to relate attentively to their students, especially to those whose theses they supervise. An attentively listening supervisor is of value, not only for those who have difficulties getting their ideas expressed, but also for those who tend to take up a lot of speaking space, for the teaching staff always influence by example. Furthermore, while supervisors may often think of their work in terms of giving advice, it can be equally important to be the unintimidating and reliable listener, to whom students can articulate their ideas—in other words, to perform Socratic midwifery without a demonstration of superiority.

4.5 The Aalborg Summer School: Feminist Political Philosophy and Problem-Based Learning

The summer school titled Feminist Political Philosophy: A Problem-Based Learning Approach, designed by Antje Gimmler, was held at Aalborg University. This summer school was somewhat smaller than the previous two had been, with twenty students, of which 70% were women. All except one of the students were from the Nordic countries.

As the title of the summer school tells us, the pedagogical point of departure of the course was problem-based learning (PBL). PBL is one of the manifestations of the pedagogical awakening that started in the 1960s and 1970s, and like feminist pedagogy and critical pedagogy, it emphasises the meaning of collective formation of knowledge, transformation through learning,[16] and student-centredness.

The motivation for using PBL in a feminist summer school was the potential of the approach to emancipate students by offering them a clear method of practising philosophy and doing research. This point of departure echoed some feminist philosophers' concerns about the vagueness of the philosophical method and the arbitrariness of the evaluations of philosophical work. Katrina Hutchison has pointed out that unlike the empirical sciences, philosophy cannot offer "data" as proof for the significance of the research, which makes identifying high standards in philosophy is difficult. She suggests that such an identification could happen through a thorough examination, articulation and teaching of methods. This would enhance the students' awareness of the different ways of approaching philosophical questions as well as their ability to see themselves as skilled practitioners (Hutchison 2013, 120).

In Aalborg University, students are encouraged to explore and experiment in their projects. However, as one of the Aalborg Summer School lecturers, Ole Ravn, put it, the method of research taught in Aalborg is not completely different from the usual research practice. Rather, the idea is to present that method very clearly and to check that the research process is working.

Even if PBL forms the pedagogical point of departure for all studies in Aalborg, there are still differences between the disciplines in how it is applied. For instance, project groups tend to be smaller in the humanities than in the natural sciences. Philosophy, of course, also differs from the natural sciences in the sense that its focus has always been on questions rather than answers. However, the idea that problems should be found "in the outside world" is different from how philosophy is often taught in universities; students are frequently encouraged to understand a problem already framed in philosophical discussions before them. The Aalborg University PBL model, which encourages students to find the problem in society, typically in the workplace, and to write their master's theses for companies and organisations, emphasises the role of applied philosophy and opens up avenues for students to find work outside academia. In this sense, Aalborg University has already responded to the need described by Robert Frodeman and Adam Briggle (2016), namely the need to introduce philosophy to a wider range of social environments.

One of the important influences on PBL, as it is currently practised at the University of Aalborg, is the work of a Danish theorist, Knud Illeris(1974) . According to him, one should rather talk about problem-*oriented* than about problem-*based* learning, for the latter is easily associated with the idea that a problem is handed over to a student by the lecturer, whereas the students should be encouraged to formulate the problems themselves (1974). From Illeris's point of view, the problem is to be found outside the disciplines, in the society, rather than within the disciplines and their idiosyncrasies. Even so, the term "problem-based learning", already quite well known as such, has not been abandoned. Instead, the Aalborg model has been redefined as *project-oriented— problem-based learning* (PO-PBL) (see e.g. Hernandez et al. 2015).

---

[16] About transformative learning, see Illeris (2014).

In Aalborg, students typically work on their projects in groups, which is quite different from the typical philosophical way of working. Hernandez, Ravn and Valero argue that group work enhances the students' abilities to co-operate (2015). In its commitment to collaborative student work, PBL resembles feminist pedagogies. Collaboration, on the other hand, differs from the emphasis on individual performance that is more common in philosophy classes. Despite the group work mode, however, students in Aalborg are assessed individually.

Due to the limited length of the Gender and Philosophy summer school as well as the dispersion of students in different countries and universities after it ended, the typical PO-PBL mode of learning of the University of Aalborg had to be modified. In other words, less time could be spent formulating problems and the student's work was more limited in scope. What is more, the written coursework was done in most cases individually, whereas group work was done mainly in discussions.

Well before the beginning of the course, the students were given access to the reading material, and they were asked to familiarise themselves with it. Some of the articles dealt with PBL while others highlighted the different aspects of feminist political philosophy: pragmatism, psychoanalysis, phenomenology, postmodernism and theory of intersectionality. Still other articles dealt with diverse topical issues in the context of gender: citizenship, torture, war, identity politics, capitalism and the Global South.

A typical day in the summer school started with a lecture, after which the students went on to discuss the reading material pertaining to the lecture in two-hour hands-on workshops. After that the students returned to the classroom to share the results of their workshop and to discuss the issues they were particularly interested in. At the end of each day, time was reserved for reflecting on the insights of that day.

During the first day of the summer school the students were initiated in PBL. The historical background of the method was discussed, as were the different phases of doing a research project. The lecturers also explained the role of one's own experience in formulating the research question: it is essential to start with one's experience, which is understood as an interaction with the environment, and to yet become aware of one's own viewpoint as limited and normative. In other words, recognition of and critical reflection on one's own viewpoint were integrated in the pedagogical approach.

After the first day, PBL remained present on the level of practice, while other topics became the explicit content of the lectures. From the second day on, feminist political philosophy was discussed from different perspectives: universalism and difference, psychoanalytic theories, violence and the perspectives of the Global South.

Before the beginning of the course the students were asked to write a short paper on their relation to feminist political philosophy. They were advised to start with their own position and to reflect upon what affects them as persons. After this they were requested to bring up one question in feminist political philosophy that they were particularly interested in and to describe the origins of their interest. They could also reflect on the ways in which the issue was present in the media and understood by the general public. In other words, the students were encouraged to reflect upon their own experience and point of departure first, and only then think of the issue at a more general level.

This assignment formed a kind of background paper for the actual coursework, but the question discussed in the actual coursework did not have to be the same as in the initial paper. In their coursework, the students were to deal with "real" issues that troubled them and to use the lectures and theory to reshape the initial issue into a problem. It was emphasised that the thought process moves back and forth between experience and theory, and that it is quite possible that one is able to properly formulate the problem only after writing the paper. However, after first formulating the problem, the students were asked to think about the means through which they could solve it. With readiness to reformulate the problem, they were able to describe the initially elusive phenomenon.

As we can see, in this process the personal experience of the student is valued and the rootedness of learning in that personal experience is highlighted. Instead of presenting the student with an abstract task of reflecting upon a theory, theories are presented as possibilities for giving shape to meaningful, real-life issues. In short, the goal of PBL is not only to help students learn, but to allow a learning process that transforms the student and makes them more in control of their own resources as thinkers.

To work towards that goal, one can use more unconventional ways of learning philosophy, some of which were dealt with in the context of feminist pedagogy. As one of the exercises related to learning the gender theory of psychoanalysis, the students were asked to form groups and take one or more photographs with a gender content that could be interpreted from the viewpoint of psychoanalysis. These photos were taken on the campus and later discussed in classroom. Exercises such as these can be inspiring as students can approach an issue from a different angle, bypassing the argumentative and source-bound side of philosophy for a while and working in a more experimental and intuitive mode.

Irrespective of the pedagogical framework (whether it is PBL or something else), the use of images can add variety to the learning process. Students can be asked to describe with an image (e.g. a photo) their attitudes to their studies or their goals. Similarly, students can be asked to describe these or other issues by choosing flashcards. The images provide a way of accessing the emotional side of their studies and generating informal discussion. Exercises of this kind, of course, require the lecturer to plan carefully beforehand not only what to teach but how to teach it, and to make decisions about the time given to and rhythm of different modes of learning during the class.

References

Airas, Maija, David Delahunty, Markus Laitinen, Marja-Liisa Saarilammi, Tuomas Sarparanta, Getuar Shemsedini, Heidi Stenberg, Hilla Vuori and Hanna Väätäinen. 2019. Taustalla on väliä: ulkomaalaistaustaiset opiskelijat korkeakoulupolulla. Karvi, julkaisut 22: 2019.

Aristotle. 2001. *Nicomachean Ethics (NE)*. Trans. W. D. Ross. Blacksburg, VA: Virginia Tech.
Bartky, Sandra Lee. 2003. A Life Sentence in Bohemia. In *Singing in the Fire: Stories of Women in Philosophy*, ed. Linda Martín Alcoff, 15–22. Lanham: Rowman and Littlefield Publishers.
Bench, Shane, Heather Lench, Jeffrey Liew, Kathi Miner and Sarah Flores. 2015. Gender Gaps in Overestimation of Math Performance. *Sex Roles* 72 (11): 536–546.
Cole, David A., Joan M. Martin, Lachan A. Peeke, A. D. Seroczynski and Jonathan Fier. 1999. Children's Over- and Underestimation of Academic Competence: A Longitudinal Study of Gender Differences, Depression, and Anxiety. *Child Development* 70 (2): 459–73
Foucault, Michel. 1990. *The History of Sexuality: Volume 2, The Use of Pleasure*. Trans. Robert Hurley. New York, NY: Vintage Books.
Fuchs, Thomas. 2012. The Phenomenology of Body Memory. In *Body Memory, Metaphor and Movement*, eds Sabine C. Koch, Thomas Fuchs, Michela Summa and Cornelia Müller, 9–22. Amsterdam: John Benjamins.
Frodeman, Robert and Briggle, Adam. 2016. *Socrates Tenured: The Institutions of 21st-Century Philosophy*. London: Rowman & Littlewood.
Gendlin, Eugene T. 1996. *Focusing-Oriented Psychotherapy: A Manual of the Experiential Method*. New York, NY: Guilford Press.
Gendlin, Eugene T. 2004. Introduction to Thinking at the Edge. In *The Folio* 9 (1).
Gendlin, Eugene T. 2007. *Focusing*. New York, NY: Bantam Books.
Gendlin, Eugene T. 2017. *Saying What We Mean: Implicit Precision and the Responsive Order. Selected Works by Eugene T. Gendlin*, eds Edward S. Casey and Donata M. Schoeller. Evanston: Northwestern University Press.
Grunspan, Daniel Z., Sarah L. Eddy, Sara A. Brownell, Benjamin L. Wiggins, Alison J. Crow and Steven M. Goodreau. 2016. Males Under-Estimate Academic Performance of Their Female Peers in Undergraduate Biology Classrooms. (Report). *PLoS One* 11 (1). http://journals.plos.org/plosone/article?id=https://doi.org/10.1371/journal.pone.0148405. Accessed 7 April 2022.
Halttunen-Riikonen, Elina. 2014. Kilpailun vai keskustelun tähden? Naisten kokemuksia filosofian opiskelusta. *Niin & näin* 21 (1): 107–110.
Heinämaa, Sara. 2000. *Ihmetys ja rakkaus: esseitä ruumiin ja sukupuolen fenomenologiasta*. Helsinki: Nemo.
Heinämaa, Sara. 2017. "Love and Admiration (Wonder): Fundaments of the Self-Other Relations." In *Emotional Experiences: Ethical and Social Significance*, eds John J. Drummond and Sonja Rinofner-Kreidl, 155–174. London: Policy Network.
Hernandez, Carola, Ole Ravn and Paola Ravino. 2015. The Aalborg University PO-PBL Model from a Socio-Cultural Learning Perspective. *Journal of Problem Based Learning in Higher Education* 3 (2): 16–36. https://journals.aau.dk/index.php/pbl/article/view/1206/993. Accessed 22 April 2022.
Hildegard Westerkamp—Inside the Soundscape/Sound Walk: https://www.hildegardwesterkamp.ca/sound/installations/Nada/soundwalk/. Accessed 2 May 2022.
hooks, bell. 1994. *Teaching to Transgress: Education as the Practice of Freedom*. New York, NY: Routledge.
hooks, bell. 2000. *Feminism Is for Everybody: Passionate Politics*. Cambridge, MA: South End Press.
Hutchison, Katrina. 2013. Sages and Cranks. The Difficulty of Identifying First-Rate Philosophers. In *Women in Philosophy: What Needs to Change?* eds Katrina Hutchison and Fiona Jenkins, 103–126. New York, NY: Oxford University Press.
Illeris, Knud. 1974. *Problemorientering og deltagerstyring*. København: Munsgaard.
Illeris, Knud. 2014. *Transformative Learning and Identity*. Abingdon, Oxon: Routledge.
Jóhannesdóttir, Guðbjörg R. and Thorgeirsdottir Sigridur. 2016. Reclaiming Nature by Reclaiming the Body. *Balkan Journal of Philosophy* 8 (1): 39–48.
Käyhkö, Mari. 2014. Kelpaanko? Riitänkö? Kuulunko? Työläistaustaiset naiset, yliopisto-opiskelu ja luokan kokemukset. *Sosiologia: Westermarck-seuran julkaisu* 51 (1): 4–20.
Lehtinen, Virpi. 2007. On Philosophical Style. *European Journal of Women's Studies* 14 (2): 109–125.

References

Mills, Charles W. 1998. *Blackness Visible: Essays on Philosophy and Race.* Ithaca, NY: Cornell University Press.

Ratcliffe, Rebecca and Claire Shaw. 2015. "Philosophy Is for Posh, White Boys with Trust Funds": Why Are There So Few Women? *The Guardian (London, England),* 5 Jan. https://www.theguardian.com/higher-education-network/2015/jan/05/philosophy-is-for-posh-white-boys-with-trust-funds-why-are-there-so-few-women. Accessed 21 April 2022.

Salamon, Gayle. 2009. Justification and Queer Method, Or Leaving Philosophy. *Hypatia* 24 (1): 225–230.

Sanchez, Carlos. 2011. Philosophy and the Post-Immigrant Fear. *Philosophy in the Contemporary World* 18 (1): 31–42.

Sveinsdóttir, Ásta. 2015. Social Construction. *Philosophy Compass* 10 (12): 884–892.

Thorgeirsdottir Sigridur. 2020. The Torn Robe of Philosophy: Philosophy as a Woman in *The Consolation of Philosophy* by Boethius. In *Methodological Reflections on Women's Contribution and Influence in the History of Philosophy,* eds Sigridur Thorgeirsdottir and Ruth Edith Hagengruber, 83–95. Cham: Springer.

Witt, Charlotte. 2011. *The Metaphysics of Gender.* Oxford, NY: Oxford University Press.

Open Access This chapter is licensed under the terms of the Creative Commons Attribution 4.0 International License (http://creativecommons.org/licenses/by/4.0/), which permits use, sharing, adaptation, distribution and reproduction in any medium or format, as long as you give appropriate credit to the original author(s) and the source, provide a link to the Creative Commons license and indicate if changes were made.

The images or other third party material in this chapter are included in the chapter's Creative Commons license, unless indicated otherwise in a credit line to the material. If material is not included in the chapter's Creative Commons license and your intended use is not permitted by statutory regulation or exceeds the permitted use, you will need to obtain permission directly from the copyright holder.

Chapter 5
The Moral Situation: Self and Other

Abstract Questions of power and ethics were implicitly present in the previous chapters. In this chapter, I deal with them in more detail, examining the power struggles in the classroom in terms of the relationship between the student and the lecturer as well as that between students. I also discuss ways out of the struggle, including a reflective attitude, classroom practices and considerations of spatial arrangements. Further, recognition, generosity and care are suggested as possible ways to overcome the difficult ethical situations in learning and teaching philosophy. In this context, I discuss the Oslo Summer School, where care ethics was used as the theoretical point of departure.

5.1 Power Struggles in the Classroom and How to Move Beyond Them

To gain an insight on your own power as a lecturer, you only need to temporarily to become a student again. At that very moment, you become aware of how many feelings rush through you during the class. Sometimes those feelings are pride, joy and inspiration, but quite often they include frustration, disappointment, humiliation and anger. When the well-meaning lecturer first encourages you, who are only a beginner in whatever you are learning, to engage in a group discussion and not to care if you make some mistakes, and only a while later uses your mistake in order to make a general point to the whole class, doesn't that feel like a smack on the face? Wouldn't you like to protest? Or, when you have prepared a short presentation about an issue that is important to you, and the lecturer, who is concerned about keeping to time, practically ignores your input, don't you feel betrayed? Furthermore, you may feel you are quite knowledgeable about a topic discussed in the class, but at the same time you feel that the discussion is lingering on basic issues, and you do not participate in the conversation, so the lecturer can move to more interesting matters. End result: the lecturer takes you for a timid beginner, who needs encouragement, and you feel extremely frustrated.

Of course, as a lecturer who temporarily is in the student's role, you are is still in a different position than a person who is a full-time student and has no pedagogical training or experience: you are not as trapped in the power dynamics between the teaching staff and the students, because you are able to evaluate the learning situation from different perspectives. However, the lecturer's position of power can hardly escape your attention. Even if the lecturer's intentions are good and their teaching methods progressive, they still hold the power to judge, the power of telling you that you are wrong or right, the right to evaluate, power over you who are a student. Other lecturers wish to assert their authority and use the classroom as a showcase of their own brilliance. This relation, in which students occupy the position of a reverent audience whereas the lecturer obtains that of a demigod, can develop regardless of the methods the lecturer uses. It is not unheard of that charismatic individuals use unconventional methods in order to gain further control over others, rather than to emancipate them.

Nevertheless, the lecturer is not the only one who possesses power in the classroom. A student can challenge the lecturer's authority, including their expertise on the topic and their ability to take into account different viewpoints—for instance, feminist, LGBTIQ+, racial, political or religious, or pertaining to a different manner of doing philosophy. Sometimes a student's question or comment may catch the lecturer off guard, and she may feel that her authority is threatened. The lecturer may be tempted to use her superior knowledge and skills in argumentation to solidify her position of power. This strategy is problematic, for the lecturer and the student are hardly equal rivals. Even in philosophy, arguments are not just arguments, but there are living, breathing, vulnerable individuals behind them, and it may serve the learning situation better if the lecturer does not continue arguing the point until the bitter end but leaves things open-ended. After all, one is not teaching just theory but is always also an example of how a philosopher relates to others, and of how a staff member relates to students. Through one's example, one can teach the students how to gain and maintain authority by undermining the viewpoints of others, or one can teach them a mode of dialogue and interaction that is tolerant of uncertainties and differences and progresses as a shared quest for increasingly nuanced understanding.

The question of hierarchy is not present only in the relationship between the lecturer and the students. Students may be involved in building hierarchies between themselves. Occupying speaking space, showing off their knowledgeability, emphasising their commitment to the practice of philosophy, forming circles of the like-minded and belittling or ignoring the input of others are some of the ways in which students may seek to establish a high-ranking position among their fellow students. Some of them may invest more in such pursuits, while others may feel frustrated with the implicit competition, or come to identify themselves as misfits or as inferior to the more knowledgeable. Yet finding one's place in the hierarchy is not necessarily reflected upon or planned but lived as a part of everyday interaction.

Given the lecturer's position as the one who frames the learning experience and is expected to provide something meaningful for the students to consider, it is hardly surprising that students sometimes compete for the lecturer's attention. Attaining that attention can have significant consequences for the student's future in academia, if the relationship between the enthusiastic student and the lecturer turns into one of academic patronage (see e.g. Nichols et al. 1985; Martin 2009).

Not all agree that such a competition should be an inbuilt feature of any system of education. hooks has suggested that the competition for the lecturer's attention reflects the competitiveness built in the capitalist economic system (1994, 199). While this may be partially true, it should not be forgotten that very early on, Plato's *Symposium* describes students competing for Socrates's attention. This may indicate that such a rivalry will not go away with the demise of capitalism.

With admirable candour, hooks analyses her own relationships with students. She points out that sometimes she is accused of becoming attached to some students of the class (1994, 198–199). Such attachments may not be altogether rare, not least because some students may be more enthusiastic about the lecturer's topic and approach them more eagerly than others. Also, personal background and temperament can explain why lecturers may become more interested in some students than others.[1] hooks's response is to ask her students to analyse why her affection for some would take anything away from the others (1994, 198–199). Nevertheless, the solution to dismiss the students' concerns about favouritism as inherent in a competitive society is not satisfactory and hardly alleviates the students' worries about not being treated equally. I suggest that a more ethical approach to the interaction between the student and the lecturer can be attained if, rather than asking the students to disregard the lecturer's more affectionate relationship with some students, as hooks suggests, the lecturer engages in self-reflective practices in their teaching, and displays sensitivity towards the diversity of the students and their needs. Another important question the teaching staff should always be aware enough to ask themselves, is: what kind of role does my sexuality play in the way I relate to students? Being flattered by the attention of some, perceiving others as rivals at least partly because of their gender—these tendencies are difficult to overcome if one denies them. Acknowledging that one can be biased in this manner, despite one's commitment to equality on the level of principles, is the first step out of practices of implicit favouritism.

Most importantly, if the lecturer consistently practises the ethics of generosity and care, that is, if the lecturer is genuinely open towards the needs of all students and shows that the input of each student is equally welcome, the students will eventually acknowledge and respond to this. The lecturer does not have to give into impulses to prefer this student to that: it is their job to become interested in the potentials and flourishing of all their students. In the long run, this attitude will be rewarded by the students' trust. Hierarchy-reducing methods can likewise prove useful in the attempt to secure equal treatment of all students: pair and group work that allow the less vocal students to become more confident to express their views, or setting a fixed time for everybody's interventions—in seminars, by actually timing those interventions or by giving each student a few chips with which they can acquire limited time to speak.

As was demonstrated by the first example in this chapter, both the lecturer and the students contribute to the emotional atmosphere of the class without being aware of

---

[1] Bridget Cooper argues that a teacher with a working-class background may find teaching pupils with a similar background particularly rewarding (2011, 73).

it. Often the given feedback is merely gestural: smiling, looking serious, frowning, looking at the other (student or staff member), ignoring them and so on. Given the phenomenon of implicit bias, the lecturer should, perhaps, pay particular attention to how they relate to women students and students belonging to other minorities.

An exaggerated reflectivity is not the ideal to be sought after in the teaching staff—it is well known that such an attitude makes all spontaneous action difficult. However, if one takes upon oneself the task of teaching, one should be genuinely interested in the student and to check one's own attitude, when something appears to be going wrong in the communication between the student and the lecturer or in the general classroom situation.

As Beauvoir argues in *The Ethics of Ambiguity* (1947), it is when one no longer feels *un*certain about the justification of one's actions that one should become concerned about it. According to her, the difference between "the tyrant" and "the man of good will" can be found in the certainty with which they relate to their own aims and actions. The tyrant "rests in the certainty of his aims", whereas the man of good will keeps asking himself: "Am I really working for the liberation of men? Isn't this end contested by the sacrifices through which I aim at it?" (Beauvoir 2003, 166; 1976, 133–134.)

It is always possible for both the lecturer and the student to become "tyrants" in the broad sense adopted by Beauvoir: a person who disregards aspects of the freedom and futurity in the other and nihilates the other's will. Talking over the other, interrupting the other, and ignoring and belittling the other's comments are strategies that hinder two-way interaction and are, in some cases, an outright attack against the other. This said, it is true that many of us engage behaviours such as talking over others and enjoy a rapid pace of discussion. However, for the communication to be dialogical, attentive listening has to be practised. Questions that reflect genuine curiosity and care have to be asked in order to allow the interaction to develop into more than a monologue.

Power struggles tend to spring up without effort, whereas undoing the effects of those struggles takes work. Space and attention have to be conscientiously allocated to those who are overwhelmed by the outpour of ideas from the mouths of others, or who, because of their different take on matters, are temporarily excluded from the discussion. It is a safe assumption that even if some people have not said anything for a half an hour, they do have things to say.

Teaching philosophy is not only about teaching how to make good arguments. It is about opening space for an intellectual curiosity, and sometimes, if a person in a position of authority puts all their efforts into showing how the student's argument fails, more is lost than gained: the space of intellectual freedom and inquiry is blocked.

I am aware that this view can be rejected out of hand by those who think that learning how to make good arguments and how to act when in a tight spot presupposes that professional philosophers be hard enough on students (see Antony 2012, 240). In my view, one is required to make a choice: either we teach students to be warriors who need to harden to do well in future combat, or we see them as participants in a shared project in which listening and encouragement are significant skills. As I see it, the latter approach, which I prefer, is not gendered nor in conflict with learning to create good arguments or even with receiving enough critical feedback.[2] This said, I realise that there are different cultures of interaction within philosophy; some of them can already be quite close to the collaborative approach I am suggesting whereas in others it will be harder to implement less combative practices.

The questions of hierarchy and communication also arise in how the physical space is used and arranged. It has been suggested that circular arrangements would diminish the power distance whereas the traditional arrangement of the lecturer on the podium and students in neat rows before them emphasises the authority of the lecturer over the students. From the point of view of learning results, however, there appears to be no one superior classroom arrangement: what works best depends on whether the learning calls for silent concentration on the topic or communication with others. Circular arrangements and groups of tables appear to facilitate communication, whereas rows facilitate concentration on individual assignments or listening to one speaker (Wannarka and Ruhl 2008).

Needless to say, architectural design affects the possibilities of interaction in the learning space (e.g. Lei 2010). In auditoriums, it is very difficult for the lecturer to move in the space freely and approach the individual students who ask questions. In this way, the spatial arrangement can incapacitate lecturers themselves. In the typical situation of a philosophy lecture, however, the lecturer is hardly ever totally immobile: especially when lecturers answer questions, their gestures reflect the process of thinking and can as such encourage the student to understand the practice of philosophy as a process of questioning that involves the whole body.

To summarise, the power dynamics of the classroom—brought about by the strivings of the lecturer, the students or even the physical space—do not have to be taken for granted or agreed to. Lecturers can use their position of power to create an atmosphere of trust, in which energy is liberated from implicit competition to collaboration and developing ideas together. It is important to remember, however, that there is a specific interplay between pedagogical methods and ethics: while certain hierarchising and competitive tendencies of the classroom are hard to undo without pedagogical methods that allow for alternative interactions to develop, pedagogical methods on their own cannot build trust among the students and between them and the lecturer. What is required from the lecturer is sensitivity, concern, genuine generosity towards the students, and an appreciation of the opportunity to philosophise together.

Above all, one should never be too sure about one's ability to take all the students into account in an adequate manner. Especially when student numbers are large, the classroom situation involves such a great diversity of experiences and individual situations that one most certainly remains ignorant of some of these. Despite the fact that some learning sessions are a far cry from glowing examples of shared flow, and may even occasionally fail, a vigilante attitude towards the classroom interaction

---

[2] By "not gendered" I mean that, according to my experience, the success of or need for this strategy does not arise from the gender of the student but rather, most students tend to have some feelings of uncertainty that need to be taken into account in teaching and supervision.

and one's own practices helps a great deal. In addition to this vigilance, the ethical demands of the classroom situation include recognition of others and a generosity towards them. These aspects of learning and teaching are discussed in the following section.

5.2 Recognition, Generosity and Care

In the philosophy class, there is always potential for a shared intellectual quest, during which the students and the lecturer are directed towards a common object of wonder, and strive together for a greater clarity, encouraging each other with their questions and interpretations.[3] This kind of shared search differs significantly from the distractedness that often characterises our discussions with others. What is more, it may help everyone involved to understand their own lives more profoundly. In the ideal case, the students do not come out of the classroom exhausted but energised, still intensely discussing the topic of the class with each other. For the lecturer, the class is then equally energising. Especially if the course deals with her particular area of expertise and interest, it provides a great opportunity for her to think together with others, who, even if temporarily, engage with her key topic for the length of the course. Passionately lived and given, learning and teaching are no longer duties but freely exchanged, a gift.

In such a case, lecturers share their passion for philosophy, inviting the others to engage in thought processes that are directed towards understanding rather than developing an expert front. The students, likewise, shake out their concerns about how they appear to others, and engage in a lively exchange of ideas. All in all, the inner movement of the participants in the learning session could, perhaps, be described as a shared orientation in the same direction, which allows individual movement between one's prior understanding and fumbling for a new grasp of the topic, drawing from the thoughts expressed by others, experiencing them as impulses to one's own associative processes.

True enough, Beauvoir describes the liberated and equal erotic relationship in a similar manner, that is, in terms of exchange, gift and passion (Beauvoir 2010, 763; 2008, 648). What we are dealing with is, of course, a kind of love, the love of wisdom, *philosophía*, and the relationship of this love to erotic love is discussed as early as Plato's *Symposium*. Yet such experiences are not restricted to learning philosophy, as hooks's descriptions reveal (1994). Rather than try to argue for the specificity of philosophy in this instance, it is perhaps more important to understand the general ethical attitude behind such learning experiences. I already mentioned the importance of the subjects' mutual recognition of each other's freedom, which is discussed, for instance, in Beauvoir's works and Axel Honneth's philosophy of recognition. Debra Bergoffen points towards yet another ethical resource in Beauvoir, namely an ethics

---

[3] For a discussion of philosophy as love and wonder see Heinämaa (2000), as well as Irigaray (1989).

5.2 Recognition, Generosity and Care

of generosity (1997, 7). In fact, generosity and the recognition of the other's freedom are tightly interwoven in Beauvoir's philosophy.

Generosity should be distinguished here from self-sacrifice and self-denial, as well as from Aristotle's description of generosity as the middle way between meanness and wastefulness (see *NE* IV:1/2001). From the Beauvoirian point of view, being generous towards others does not imply nihilation of the self, nor does it reflect a "moderate" attitude towards consumption and wealth. Instead, generous giving does not imply losing anything or asking for something in return. This conception of generosity resembles the one Friedrich Nietzsche puts forward in *Thus Spake Zarathustra* (1883–1885/2009). Both Nietzsche and Beauvoir argue that genuine generosity does not operate within the sphere of bargaining or commerce.[4] When things such as appreciation, adoration and loyalty are asked for in return, an act does not demonstrate generosity.[5] Beauvoir's idea is that generosity can only operate when the other's freedom is recognised, and if I wish to control the other's actions, thinking that he owes me, I did not really give him a gift but a loan, or what is even worse, I was initially motivated by my own vanity and will to gain power over the other, to be his tyrant—which is the exact opposite of true generosity (see Beauvoir 2003, 277–278; 2004b, 123–124).[6] The only thing the benefactor can ask of the other is the recognition of freedom in the act of giving (Beauvoir 2003, 277; 2004b, 123;).

While Beauvoir's ethics of generosity is at best implicit, numerous authors have developed such ethics during the past few decades, relying not only on the work of Beauvoir or Nietzsche but also of Marcel Mauss, Georges Bataille and Emmanuel Levinas (see e.g. Bergoffen 1997; Schrift 1997, ed.; Diprose 2002). In the context of this volume it is not possible to investigate these developments in more detail, so I content myself with commenting on the possibilities of an attitude of generosity in the context of learning and teaching philosophy. A generous attitude towards the other is caring but not patronising, and as it involves the recognition of the other as free, it tends to inspire a similar attitude in others. My stinginess, in contrast, can inflict a need on others to guard their boundaries and possessions. As I pointed out earlier, both students and the faculty are in many ways vulnerable in the classroom, and it is all too easy to withdraw to the attitude of indifference and detachment when one feels threatened.

I do not propose the mere identification of generosity as a basis for ethical action would suffice to deal with all possible moral problems. There will certainly be situations in which generosity is not enough, and in which self-protection and self-care become an issue. In the context of care ethics, which, like ethics of generosity, focuses

---

[4] For an analysis of Nietzsche's conception of gift-giving and generosity, see White (2016).

[5] Beauvoir writes: "The sick man requires care; I give it to him; he recovers. But the health he recovers through me is not a good if I stop him at that. It becomes a good thing only if he makes something of it." (Beauvoir 2004, 121; 2003, 272–273.).

[6] Beauvoir's way of conceiving gift and generosity resembles Marcel Mauss's and Georges Bataille's discussion of gift and excess in that it challenges utilitarian ethics and the idea of an economy driven by self-interest. The difference lies in Beauvoir's idea that genuine generosity does not require reciprocation. In contrast to this, Mauss and Bataille argue that the *exchange* of gifts is the glue that holds the archaic society together.

on relationality, Pettersen has elaborated on Carol Gilligan's concept of mature care (Pettersen 2008, 133–150; 2011). For Pettersen, mature care involves equal care for oneself and the other (2011, 56).

Care ethics is a relatively new ethical theory, the starting points of which are usually located in Gilligan's *In a Different Voice* (1982) and Nel Noddings's *Caring* (1986/2013). Both authors suggested that women enter into ethics from a different point than men. Challenging deontological and utilitarian ethics, they argued that it was more typical for women to think of ethical choices in terms of relationality and care than through rights, rules or justice. Care itself has been defined in a number of different ways. Among the best-known is Joan Tronto's categorisation of care into: (1) attentiveness (as an inclination to become aware of need), (2) responsibility (responding to need), (3) competence (ability to provide good care) and (4) responsiveness (feeling with the other and recognition of the possibility of abuse in care) (Tronto 1993, 126–136). Care ethicists emphasise the virtual universality of the experience of care: practically all people know what it is to receive and give care, and can thereby extend their narrow self-centred horizons towards the experience of others and a concern for their well-being (e.g. Pettersen 2011, 58; Clark 2010, 150). As we can see, Tronto's definition of care does not presuppose that care should be understood as an exclusively female approach to ethics. In this sense, even though the first expressions of care ethics incorporated assumptions that can be criticised of essentialising gender, the whole of the care ethical project needs not be confined to an essentialist framework.

As Pettersen has suggested (2011, 59), the care ethical concerns and concepts are in many ways compatible with Beauvoir's ethical concerns, which were briefly discussed above. Both care ethics and existentialist ethics recognise the ambiguity of lived experience and the difficulty of making ethical decisions merely on the basis of abstract rules, while at the same time advocating systematic reasoning in the service of ethics. Yet another similarity is suspicion about the ethical value of absolute self-denial in favour of others (see Pettersen 2011, 59–60). As Pettersen puts it, sometimes "the devoted carer is exploited and injured, and sometimes she inflicts harm on others in the name of care" (ibid., 60). Beauvoir in turn points out that the acts of a benefactor towards the protégé can be tyrannical, when they imply an attempt to control the other. Similar relationships of oppression can take place between lovers, spouses, and parents and children—in all of these cases one can in bad faith inflict pain on others and oneself while pretending to act for the good of others (Beauvoir 2010, e.g. 201, 208; 2008, 302, 312). In the classroom, too, devotion to the other can be, at its basis, a form of control, a desire to possess the affection and appreciation of the other.

This concern for the possible abuse of care that harms oneself and others, is related to the concept of mature care. According to Pettersen, the notion of mature care, first introduced by Gilligan, is of particular interest, because it helps us to understand care as "a relational process in which both the carer and the caree participate" and in which each participant engages in promoting the flourishing of all parties as well as preventing harm to all parties (Pettersen 2011, 55).

On rare occasions, the lecturer may enter conflict situations in which the general ethical rules of academic learning and teaching are questioned by a student, who suggests that the lecturer should adopt their own case-specific justifications for adequate performance as a guiding principle. In reality, of course, each case cannot be considered as if it were the only one, for evaluation and teaching in general are preconditioned by rules of fairness and quality of academic learning. Yet, as we saw in the earlier discussion of Beauvoir's ethics, an ethically vigilant person is always ready to question their own motives. Even when the motives of the other seem questionable, the other's vulnerability opens up this possibility to us, and, along with it, introduces often painful considerations about justifying our actions. Nevertheless, this possibility of pain and worrying is also a demonstration that we have not become unable to see and feel the source of ethics in the possible suffering of the other.

From a Levinasian point of view, justice and fairness, which come to limit our responsibilities to the other, are introduced by the presence of the third party (Levinas 1999). Considering Pettersen's discussion of mature care, we can see that it is not only the third party—in this case the other real and potential students and through them the ideals of academic education—that limits our responsibilities, but also our own vulnerability and needs. Nor should we ever overlook the potential of the institutional community to solve conflict situations through collectively instituted rules and procedures.

While Foucault's concept "care of the self" (1988) is not inherently linked with care ethics, it reveals yet another aspect of care. Foucault's concept of "care of the self" refers to the introspective self-government and practices that nurture individual growth, which, according to him, were embraced by ancient Greek and Roman thinkers. We have already discussed the meaning of self-reflection in pedagogy at length, but here the focus is different: we are searching not for only good teaching practices but for a life-long development and nurture of the self, which help us interact with others in an ethical way. Today, we are often lacking such a long-term understanding of our relationship with the world, and our feeble attempts to find a more profound basis for our lives are more often channelled through commercially geared self-help practices or religion than through philosophy. Beyond the pursuit of academic accomplishments, however, the practice of philosophy itself could contribute to a specific care of the self. This kind of care could help us to act more constructively in conflicts and other challenging situations.

5.3 The Oslo Summer School: Care Ethics and Conflicts

The last of the summer schools, titled Care Ethics and Conflicts, was organised at the University of Oslo by Pettersen. 75% of the twenty-four participants were women. Most of the students were from Nordic universities.

During the course, care and conflicts were discussed from a variety of perspectives, namely in relation to private and professional relationships, war and peace, global relations, and nature. Through these perspectives, the course demonstrated that care ethics may be applied to far broader issues than is often the case: all of human interaction and even beyond.[7]

Fittingly with the theme of the summer school, the pedagogical principles were motivated by care ethical concerns. The goal was to address the diversity of students in a manner that considers their individual needs, inclinations and learning strategies. One of the leading principles was to create a non-judgemental environment in which it feels safe to both express one's ideas and to be quiet, and in which both students and lecturers are able to listen to each other attentively and respond to each other in a respectful, caring and benevolent manner. In addition, students were invited to reflect upon the role of experiences, emotions and reason in philosophy and ethics, and to self-reflection in the sense of both reflecting upon their own approaches and their reactions to the discussed topics. This way the emotional and relational aspects of learning were integrated into reasoning processes. What is more, attention was paid to the fact that the cases and dilemmas typical to care ethics can in many cases be difficult to deal with emotionally, depending on the personal history of the individual.

It was pointed out to the students that the cases care ethics analyses are not hypothetical problems made for intellectual exercises only, but actual cases that often involve pain and suffering. Not least for this reason, students were encouraged to be reflective about their experiences during the class as well as about the different points departures of others.

As we can see, the approach adopted in this summer school differed from that of the mode that is common in the teaching of philosophy. Firstly, particular attention was paid to the role of emotions in the teaching and learning processes. Secondly, instead of resorting to thought experiments, the messiness of everyday life and its moral challenges were brought into the analysis. In this way, the course addressed two complaints that philosophy students have proposed: that there is no room for emotions in philosophy and that philosophy is often understood as a game-like, empty exercise of reason (see Chap. 4).

On the practical level, the diversity of students was addressed in a number of ways, perhaps the most important being the diversity of teaching methods. The idea was to create a space that would accommodate both sociability and withdrawal. The days of the summer school consisted of lectures, group work, student presentations, structured debates and more informal discussions. At the end of each day, the students engaged in quiet work, writing their reflections on the day in a journal.

An approach that makes space for silence is quite different from what hooks suggests, as she insists that all her students have to speak, even if they did it in sign language, as has sometimes been the case in her classes (1994). It is perhaps worth noting that lecturers are often surprised by the results when the course essays are returned: it is not rare that the most talkative of the students do not write the most thought-out essays. Some students may need peace and quiet to process their thoughts, whereas others may have difficulties forming their thoughts in writing and prefer to proceed through discussion. As we saw earlier, these skills are in some

---

[7] For a discussion of the widening range of care ethics, see Pettersen 2011, 51–52.

cases related to social class, so from the viewpoint of social equality it is particularly important to make room for differences (see Sect. 4.2).

It is well known, of course, that the theories of learning styles have been hotly debated, and it is not my intention here to take a stand on these theories as such (see Pashler et al. 2008; Husmann and O'Loughlin 2019). Rather, the point of departure in the Oslo Summer School was not only to acknowledge the differences between the needs of different students but also to cater for the fact that each student needs a variety of learning methods. For instance, although people engage in social interaction with different levels of enthusiasm, after three hours of engaging in an "extrovert" or "conscientious" behaviour, all would feel tired to some extent (Leikas and Ilmarinen 2016). For this reason, all students may benefit from engaging in a variety of learning approaches during the day.

What else can one do to support withdrawing or reserved students, keeping in mind the possible sources of alienation for women students and students of other minorities? The answer need not be complicated, even if exclusions and alienations are manifold. Support can consist of encouragement and classroom strategies that create space for those who may not be so quick to verbalise their views or self-assured enough to air their views without questioning the need for this. The needed encouragement may be noticing the person individually also outside the classroom, commenting on their work in an encouraging manner, all in all demonstrating that they are worthy interlocutors and have valuable things to say.

Versatile classroom strategies can include exercises in which students move gradually from solitary work (for instance, writing down personal ideas and experiences related to a specific topic) to a group discussion, in which group members' ideas and experiences are discussed on a more general level, and finally to sharing the results with the whole class. One can distribute speaking time more democratically by limiting the times each person can speak. This can help those students who tend to take a long time to get to their actual point, to think through what they want to say before they say it. It may also be helpful if the nature of the dialogue students and lecturers want to create is discussed explicitly at the beginning of the course. When students participate in setting the rules of the interaction, this makes it easier for them to create a reflective relationship to the rules.

Sometimes students can benefit from learning a theory, such as feminist theory, that thematises their particular position and allows them to become rooted within their field, instead of being left adrift. As was suggested in Sect. 3.4, providing a discussion of the history of women thinkers can help women students to become rooted in philosophy.

References

Antony, Louise. 2012. Different Voices or Perfect Storm: Why Are There So Few Women in Philosophy? *Journal of Social Philosophy*, 43 (3), 227–255.
Aristotle. 2001. *Nicomachean Ethics (NE)*. Trans. W. D. Ross. Blacksburg, VA: Virginia Tech.
Beauvoir, Simone de. 1947. *Pour une morale de l'ambiguïté*. Paris: Gallimard. English edition: Beauvoir, Simone de. 1976. *The Ethics of Ambiguity* (trans. Frechtman, Bernard). New York: Citadel Press.
Beauvoir, Simone de. 2008. *Le deuxième sexe II : L'expérience vécue*. Paris: Gallimard. English edition: Beauvoir, Simone de. 2010. *The Second Sex* (trans. Borde, Constance and Malovany-Chevallier, Sheila). New York: Alfred A. Knopf.
Bergoffen, Debra B. 1997. *The Philosophy of Simone De Beauvoir: Gendered Phenomenologies, Erotic Generosities*. Albany, NY: State University of New York Press.
Clark Miller, Sarah. 2010. Cosmopolitan Care. *Ethics and Social Welfare* 4 (2): 145–157.
Cooper, Bridget. 2011. *Empathy in Education: Engagement, Values and Achievement*. London: Continuum.
Diprose, Rosalyn. 2002. *Corporeal Generosity: On Giving with Nietzsche, Merleau-Ponty, and Levinas*. Albany, NY: SUNY Press.
Foucault, Michel. 1988. *The History of Sexuality: Volume 3, The Care of the Self*. Trans. Robert Hurley. New York, NY: Vintage Books.
Gilligan, Carol. 1982. *In a Different Voice: Psychological Theory and Women's Development*. Cambridge, Mass.: Harvard University Press.
Heinämaa, Sara. 2000. *Ihmetys ja rakkaus: esseitä ruumiin ja sukupuolen fenomenologiasta*. Helsinki: Nemo.
hooks, bell. 1994. *Teaching to Transgress: Education as the Practice of Freedom*. New York, NY: Routledge
Husmann, Polly R. and Valerie Dean O'Loughlin. 2019. Another Nail in the Coffin for Learning Styles? Disparities among Undergraduate Anatomy Students' Study Strategies, Class Performance, and Reported VARK Learning Styles. *Anatomical Sciences Education*, 12 (1), pp. 6–19.
Irigaray, Luce. 1989. *Éthique de la différence sexuelle*. Collection Critique. Paris: Minuit.
Lei, Simon A. 2010. Classroom Physical Design Influencing Student Learning and Evaluations of College Instructors: A Review of Literature. *Education*, Sep 22, 128.
Leikas, Sointu and Ville-Juhani Ilmarinen. 2016. Happy Now, Tired Later? Extraverted and Conscientious Behavior Are Related to Immediate Mood Gains, but to Later Fatigue. *Journal of Personality* 85 (5).
Levinas, Emmanuel. 1999. *Otherwise than Being or Beyond Essence*. Trans. Alphonso Lingis. Pittsburgh, PA: Duquesne University Press.
Martin, Brian. 2009. Academic Patronage. *International Journal for Educational Integrity* 5 (1): 3–19.
Nichols, Irene A., Holly M. Carter and M. Patricia Golden. 1985. The Patron System in Academia: Alternative Strategies for Empowering Academic Women. *Women's International Forum* 8 (4), 383–390. http://www.sciencedirect.com/science/article/pii/0277539585900202. Accessed 22 April 2022.
Nietzsche, Friedrich. 2009. *Thus Spake Zarathustra: A Book For All and None*. Trans. Thomas Common. Auckland: The Floating Press.
Noddings, Nel. 2013. *Caring: A Relational Approach to Ethics and Moral Education*. Berkeley: University of California Press.
Pashler, Harold, Mark McDaniel, Doug Rohrer and Robert Bjork. 2008. Learning Styles: Concepts and Evidence. *Psychological Science in the Public Interest*, 9 (3), 105–119.
Pettersen, Tove. 2008. *Comprehending Care*. Lanham, MD: Lexington Books.
Pettersen, Tove. 2011. The Ethics of Care: Normative Structures and Empirical Implications. *Health Care Analysis* 19 (1): 51–64.
Schrift, Alan D. (ed.). *The Logic of the Gift: Towards an Ethic of Generosity*.

References

Tronto, Joan C. 1993. *Moral Boundaries: A Political Argument for an Ethic of Care*. New York: Routledge.

Wannarka, Rachel and Kathy Ruhl. 2008. Seating Arrangements that Promote Positive Academic and Behavioural Outcomes: A Review of Empirical Research. *Support for Learning* 23 (2): 89–93.

White, Richard. 2016. Nietzsche on Generosity and the Gift-Giving Virtue. *British Journal for the History of Philosophy* 24 (2): 348–364.

Open Access This chapter is licensed under the terms of the Creative Commons Attribution 4.0 International License (http://creativecommons.org/licenses/by/4.0/), which permits use, sharing, adaptation, distribution and reproduction in any medium or format, as long as you give appropriate credit to the original author(s) and the source, provide a link to the Creative Commons license and indicate if changes were made.

The images or other third party material in this chapter are included in the chapter's Creative Commons license, unless indicated otherwise in a credit line to the material. If material is not included in the chapter's Creative Commons license and your intended use is not permitted by statutory regulation or exceeds the permitted use, you will need to obtain permission directly from the copyright holder.

Chapter 6
Conclusions and Further Questions

Abstract This concluding chapter consists of three parts: the general conclusions of the whole book, "questions to ask oneself" and a discussion of the possibilities for renewing philosophy in the current state of university politics. Furthermore, the first part includes suggestions for empirical research on the underrepresentation of women in philosophy. The purpose of the second part is to help lecturers to think through their own teaching practices and possible shortcomings from the viewpoint of inclusiveness. In the third part, I ask what kind of politics could replace the neoliberal framework that has dominated the academic world for the past few decades.

6.1 General Conclusions

Women students are not as such outsiders in philosophy. They are a part of a companionship that can be rewarding in a number of ways. Just like men who practise philosophy, also women feel passionate about it, and sharing this passion with others regardless of their gender is certainly one of the joys of philosophy. Nor has it been my goal to argue that co-operation between women themselves would be unproblematic or free from power struggles: regardless of the ingroups we belong to and regardless of the fact that some of these groups may be more or less overtly discriminated against in society, within these groups, we can still enter different kinds of hierarchies and oppressive relationships.

Yet, as I have demonstrated, belonging to a minority in philosophy brings its own challenges, especially considering that philosophy has such a long history of being defined by the styles of interaction of the majority and that it still operates, to a high degree, by discussing a "canon" of texts written by members of a specific group with typical features of social class, race and gender identity. Women have participated in this companionship since the very early days, but very little of their contributions has been preserved continuously until today.

This is unfortunate, for a historical "we" of women in philosophy is missing. A great part of the history of philosophy fails to present women as philosophising subjects. Quite often, women are objectified and disparaged, as if they were an alien and inferior species. To compound this, many women feel that the image of the philosopher is not something they can relate to, and the tacit rules of the philosophy class and interaction between students can appear arbitrary or unsatisfactory. The masculine ideal of the philosopher genius can seem impossible to attain even if women students do well in their studies. Loving philosophy as a mode of thinking and enjoying its breadth and depth do not necessarily coincide with feeling at home in the social practices of the discipline. From the viewpoint of many, it appears that philosophy somehow minimises the significance of embodiment and expression of emotions in favour of reason, as if these two could not coexist.

I do not claim that all women students everywhere share these experiences, nor that women are the only ones to experience these modes of estrangement. As long as many individuals share some of these feelings, however, there is a reason to find appropriate ways to renew philosophy teaching, and even to think through the very goals of philosophy. In what kinds of contexts and companionships should we aim to practise philosophy in the future?

In the Gender and Philosophy summer schools, diverse strategies were used to promote inclusiveness: alternative ways of teaching the history of philosophy, problem-based learning, engaging the senses, and cultivation of care and generosity in the classroom. As I have suggested, there is no magic wand with which one could conjure up an equal and non-discriminatory learning environment out of the complex, competitive reality of academia. However, I have emphasised the significance of ethics in education: vigilance in the learning situation and sensitivity to the needs of the students. In addition, it is pivotal for lecturers to acknowledge their own biases and possibly stereotypical ways of interacting with students. At the same time, as Pettersen's conception of mature care suggests, lecturers have to remain sensitive to their own needs and not be taken in by the chance to act as idols or omnipotent benefactors, with all the impossible demands these roles bring along.

The study at hand has raised numerous issues calling for empirical research. To understand the varying degrees to which women students become interested in philosophy, it would be of interest to investigate attitudes to and teaching of philosophy in upper secondary school, and to compare the success experienced by female and male students in their philosophy courses with their identification with the subject. It would be equally important to acquire more data on the sources of alienation from philosophy, the background for choosing a main subject, and the importance of factors such as the reputation or location of the university and any regional differences in the general interest in philosophy of women applicants.

The question of regional factors brings us back to the regional differences in the upper secondary school education in philosophy, not forgetting the possible regional impact on the applicants' values and perception of the gendered aspects of different disciplines. When students apply to a university, they may have a poor conception of how the theoretical emphasis of a specific department may affect their feeling at home as a student in that department, and more general ideas about the university and one's chances of being accepted to study there may have a lot of weight with applicants when they choose an institution.

Quantitative studies can help map out some aspects of these issues, but they leave a deeper layer of the student experience virtually intact. Interviews can provide a much richer understanding, not least because interviewees can elucidate experiences that the researcher might not think to ask about in a questionnaire. If women's underrepresentation in philosophy is researched further, an approach that combines quantitative and qualitative methods might be particularly useful.

Students' socialisation into philosophy would be yet another interesting theme for a qualitative study. Eager to integrate into the philosophical community, philosophy students may be disposed to take for granted the social demands and values of the field, which, for historical reasons, have been formed according to the needs and social styles of a fairly homogenous group – mainly White, heterosexual cis men. More general research on the possible formation of homosociality in philosophy, how philosophy in this sense compares to other male-dominated fields, and how its social norms may yield in heterosocial situations, might shed light on the feelings of belonging and not-belonging, or inclusion and alienation, within philosophy.

It is not rare for academics to think that the topic they teach is more important than how it is taught. Learning about pedagogy seems to steal time from something more important, namely the content of research and teaching. However, just as learning about philosophy can free our thinking in general, learning about pedagogy can free our teaching. Naturally, not every lecturer needs to use exactly the same methods. The goal is not to conform to a specific pedagogical framework but to gain more latitude in one's teaching practices and make the learning experience more rewarding for the students with the means that go well with the lecturer's own abilities, aspirations and characteristics.

To support the reader's strivings, however, I propose below a checklist which can be used as an aid to inclusive teaching of philosophy. I prefer to present the checklist as a list of questions to ask oneself—firstly, because often there are no easy yes-or-no solutions to practical problems in the classroom, and secondly, because I believe that both philosophy and pedagogy operate best not by following orders, but by means of dialogue, questioning and reflection. This said, the choice of questions and the suggestions related to them certainly carry some normative elements, based on what I consider to be central for inclusive teaching.

6.2 Questions to Ask Oneself

Some of the following questions could be applied to promote inclusive teaching of any subject, while others are more philosophy-specific. In any case, if not every day, at least every now and then, it is worth asking oneself:

- Do I listen to my students attentively? If some of them are insecure or feel alienated from their studies in philosophy because of their gender, ethnicity, race, disability or class, do I have the means to encourage them?

- As a supervisor, do I listen to my supervisees and encourage them or do I just tell them what to do and what is wrong with their work? Do I engage in thinking together with them?
- Do I have a policy for making it easier for women students and students belonging to other minorities to feel at home in philosophy? For instance, do I discuss the work of women and Black philosophers? If I feel incompetent in these topics, do I at the minimum have a strategy to make the work of those philosophers visible and available to interested students?
- Have I acquired some basic knowledge of the complexity regarding the issues of gender and sexuality? Should I familiarise myself with the experience of trans women and men and gender-non-conforming individuals?
- Am I ready to check my own assumptions of what is relevant in the history of philosophy? Do I have enough knowledge about the different strategies of integrating minorities into the teaching of the history of philosophy?
- When I give examples, am I aware of their gendered aspects? Which variations of examples would surpass the usual White, heterosexual cis male, able-bodied norm?
- Do I offer stereotypical or counter-stereotypical examples of "important philosophers"? Do I lend support to the idea of the philosopher as a lone wolf or as a suffering genius, or should I challenge this stereotype?
- Am I familiar with concepts such as "micro-inequity", "implicit bias" and "stereotype threat"? Do I have strategies for avoiding these phenomena?
- What are the implicit practices of the proposed learning environments in philosophy and how do they shape the possibilities of diverse students? Should these practices be made explicit? Should I be involved in their development or help students themselves make choices pertaining to them?
- Am I able to see the possibilities for individual philosophical flourishing in all students? Is my inability to encourage some students intertwined with my difficulty interact with that particular gender or race?
- Am I sensitive enough about when to discuss differences of class, gender, ethnicity, ability and so on, and when not to draw attention to these?
- Do I have a constructive policy of how to act if students in my class engage in subtle discriminatory practices, for instance, if they show appreciation only to comments from their own ingroup and disregard the speaking space of others? If finger-pointing is a bad strategy, can I change the group dynamics in more subtle ways?
- Is the classroom harassment-free?
- Am I aware of my own power and possibilities as a lecturer or do I find myself silently blaming the students if something goes wrong in the classroom? How do I overcome situations in which I am challenged by my students? Do I find ways to build trust between them and myself or do I simply appeal to my authority?
- Are some of the students sexualised or racialised? Do I myself engage in such practices? Do I refer to students as representatives of a specific gender identity, race or religion or do I allow them to be learners among others, without unwarranted assumptions about their outlooks on life?

- How do my own insecurities reflect on my teaching? If it is impossible and not even desirable to lose all insecurities, can acknowledging them help me to begin dealing with them?
- Am I aware of the ways in which emotions can be shut out of a philosophy class? Do I allow space for discussing personal experience? Do I consciously encourage learning strategies that integrate the student's emotions and past in the learning process?
- Am I, however, aware that as a lecturer I am not a therapist and that I need to protect myself from emotional overload?
- Am I aware that not all learning experiments will succeed—that experimenting with new ways of teaching and learning presupposes a tolerance for occasional failures?
- Am I aware of the fact that in academia, a narrowly defined point of departure is often presented as neutral? Do I give the students tools to recognise this bias?
- Do I help the students to recognise the power dynamics within academia and in the classroom?
- Am I aware of my point of departure and both of my privileges and those aspects of my identity that marginalise me? Do I acknowledge the complicated reality of intersecting differences in the students?
- Do I have a policy about whether to use trigger warnings, when to use them and when not?
- Have I found the ways of teaching that work best for me and that help me most efficiently engage my students in their diversity? Am I at my best giving lectures, or would more interactive ways of teaching and learning work better in my case?

While some of the issues discussed above are relevant regardless of the time in history we are living in, it is equally true that the problems of philosophy do not develop in a vacuum. The environment in which the teaching staff and students of our time make their choices is the contemporary academia. During the past decades, universities have been increasingly driven by neoliberal politics and its carrot-and-stick approach. The very last question I want to raise on the topic of learning and teaching philosophy is about the meaning this political framework for our work.

6.3 Philosophy and the Politics of Education: What's Next?

In recent years, neoliberal university politics have merged with meritocratic practices to produce what Foucault (1977) would have called docile bodies: bodies that have internalised control and act with an almost robotic precision to achieve the goals set by the highly organised, competitive and hierarchical system. Universities in different parts of the world have faced the demands of neoliberal politics in different degrees, but in most cases the means to attain a more "efficient" and "productive" academic environment are similar: politics of austerity, attempts to decrease the number of universities and academic disciplines particularly in the humanities, attempts to gradually introduce term fees into universities that were earlier completely free of charge, privatisation, growing influence of non-academics on university boards, competition for private funding, brand development, constant changes in the organisation structure and teaching, and precarity of work.

The meritocratic tendencies of academic life have been harnessed to serve the needs of neoliberal politics by making the universities, research groups and individual researchers constantly compete for shrinking funds. Excellence is presented as the criterion for winning the competition for funding, and numerous ways of measuring this excellence are created, often with the idea to incorporate assessment of both quality and quantity. For instance, one of the most important criteria for evaluating a researcher's competence is the number of publications in high-standard peer-reviewed international journals. Even master's students may be painfully aware of the fact that in order to attain research or teaching positions, they should efficiently collect credits towards their degree, with the highest possible grades, thus creating the image of a prospective doctoral student.

A system based on the accumulation of merits and their evaluation by peers could be, in principle, woman-friendly and gender-inclusive, provided that all the necessary precautions against implicit bias had been taken into account and forms of discrimination like stereotype threat and micro-inequities had somehow been ruled out of the picture. In a meritocratic system, which academia appears to represent par excellence, the most talented and the most industrious individuals are ideally rewarded, which in turn means that basically women with excellent merits would be equal with men with excellent merits in the competition for advancement, first in their studies and then in their careers.[1]

The problem is, of course, that even though a degree of rivalry appears to have always been present in the practice of European philosophy, the demands of constant competition for the utmost merits, efficacy and production under pressure are quite far removed from the reasons why people want to learn philosophy in the first place. In other words, there is a fundamental tension between philosophy as a production of knowledge and philosophy as an attempt to genuinely engage with the world around us and with each other in the attitude of wonder. At the same time, at least half-hearted adoption of values of efficacy and production appears to be the price that one has to pay for a career in academia. If women were, indeed, to acquire a steadier foothold within philosophy, we would still be faced with the question whether there is anything left in the practice of philosophy within the constraints of the neoliberal university politics that is worth pursuing.

If we direct our gazes towards students who have chosen to study philosophy in the hope that it is a quest for wisdom, it seems obvious that the competitive framework provided by contemporary academia hardly helps them grow as human beings or to become, through this growth, better philosophers. Frodeman and Briggle have suggested that instead of deploring the current state of academia we should embrace it as a chance for a rejuvenation of philosophy (2016). As they interpret the situation, academic philosophy has long ago cut its ties with problems that people actually

---

[1] For accounts of meritocracy, see Young (1963) and Jenkins (2013).

experience as meaningful and become a hermetic inquiry into questions that have no significance outside the department. In their view, the answer to the crisis is to relinquish philosophy as defined merely in terms of academic professionalism, to bring it into contact with real issues, and to turn the classroom into a laboratory of pedagogical experimentation. As they see it, it should be the goal of philosophers to take matters into their own hands to produce a reformation of philosophy rather than just to adjust to the change that is imposed upon them from the outside. (Frodeman and Briggle 2016).

It is obvious that in our times, riddled with the rise of anti-intellectualism and populism along with overt misogyny and racism, it is rather natural and necessary for philosophers to start discussing philosophy in a closer connection with current political and ecological developments. In other words, a new philosophical orientation towards the surrounding world may not become urgent as a result of the crisis of philosophy, but rather the social, environmental and health crises of a global scope awaken philosophers to re-evaluate their goals. A shift of this nature has already begun.

The fact is that working within academia—whatever its imperfections—has until now provided philosophers with at least some security and freedom. Therefore, it is not sufficient to find out how to broaden the scope of philosophy outside academia, and what kinds of demands this broadening may bring to the teaching of philosophy—it is necessary also to find ways to develop philosophy and its teaching within academia. In the case of women, in particular, it is hardly satisfactory to show them a way out of academic philosophy at the moment their foothold within it is still insecure. For this reason, we still have to find ways to change academia from within and strive for a politics of education that has more humane values than those of meritocracy and neoliberalism. Solidarity, generosity and care do not come about because the environment in which we work or study is geared to nurture them, but because of the conscious choices we make within the limits given to us, and because of our willingness to push those limits.

This said, profound changes in social atmosphere are not only the handiwork of strong-minded individuals but, perhaps more than anything, the effect of outside forces and crisis situations. These can shake up our world and even the belief of politicians in the neoliberal agenda in an abrupt manner, as we have come to see in the context of wars, the COVID-19 pandemic and—perhaps to a lesser degree—the acceleration of climate change. Crisis situations both provide a new perspective on our possibilities for action and show us the basic human ways to seek escape from a stressful reality: denial, protest, scapegoating, panic, irrationalism, intellectualisation, withdrawal, bonding, solidarity. In such situations thinking, instead of simply reacting, is difficult, because it presupposes an intellectual space, a minimal distance to the fears we are facing.

Philosophers, too, engage in these strategies of escape. The difference is that it is our task to protect intellectual freedom: not by producing noise, propaganda, rash conclusions or quick fixes, but by creating the time and space to pause in the face of uncertainty. Ideally, the philosophy class can act as an incubator for non-tribalist thinking that counteracts the logic of hatred. How to take this legacy forward and to renew it with a sensitivity to gender, is a question to which all of us, all philosophers, should give serious thought.

References

Foucault, Michel. 1977. *Discipline and Punish: The Birth of the Prison*. London: Penguin Books.
Frodeman, Robert and Adam Briggle. 2016. *Socrates Tenured: The Institutions of 21st-Century Philosophy*. London: Rowman & Littlewood.
Jenkins, Fiona. 2013. Singing the Post-Discrimination Blues: Notes for a Critique of Academic Meritocracy. In *Women in Philosophy: What Needs to Change*, eds Hutchison Katrina and Fiona Jenkins, 81–102. Oxford: Oxford University Press.
Young, Michael. 1963. *The Rise of the Meritocracy 1870–2033: An Essay on Education and Equality*. Harmondsworth: Penguin Books.

Open Access This chapter is licensed under the terms of the Creative Commons Attribution 4.0 International License (http://creativecommons.org/licenses/by/4.0/), which permits use, sharing, adaptation, distribution and reproduction in any medium or format, as long as you give appropriate credit to the original author(s) and the source, provide a link to the Creative Commons license and indicate if changes were made.

The images or other third party material in this chapter are included in the chapter's Creative Commons license, unless indicated otherwise in a credit line to the material. If material is not included in the chapter's Creative Commons license and your intended use is not permitted by statutory regulation or exceeds the permitted use, you will need to obtain permission directly from the copyright holder.

Index

A
Able-bodiedness, 21
Academic patronage, 75
Aesara, 30
Affection, 75, 80
Alienation, 3, 4, 13–15, 19, 22–25, 34, 49, 52, 55–57, 60, 61, 64, 83, 88, 89
Analytic philosophy, 3, 7
Arendt, Hannah, 35
Aristotle, 37, 40, 44, 45, 49, 50, 79
Aspasia of Miletus, 31
Astell, Mary, 43, 44
Attentive listening, 66, 76

B
Barre, Poulain de la, 44
Bataille, Georges, 79
Battersby, Christine, 36
Beauvoir, Simone de, 4, 45, 78, 79
Bergès, Sandrine, 44
Bergoffen, Debra, 78
Black feminism, 58
Butler, Judith, 40

C
Canon, philosophical, 13, 23, 34, 36, 37, 41, 43, 44
Capitalism, 68, 75
Care
    ethics, 14, 23, 73, 79–82
    mature, 80, 81, 88
    of the self, 81
Cavendish, Margaret, 43
Châtelet, Émilie du, 43

Christine de Pizan, 19, 33, 44
Cisgender, 15
Consciousness raising, 20
Conway, Anne, 43
Cooper, Bridget, 75
Crates, 30–33
Crenshaw, Kimberlé, 20
Cudworth Masham, Damaris, 43
Cynics, 30, 31

D
Derrida, Jacques, 25
Descartes, René, 43
Deslauriers, Marguerite, 44
Dotson, Kristie, 12, 56
Du Bois, W. E. B., 24

E
Early women philosophers, 41, 42
Elisabeth of Bohemia, 43
Embodiment
    disembodiment, 59, 60
    docile bodies, 91
    lived body, 65
Epictetus, 30
Epicurus, 30
Eurocentrism, 46
Existentialism, 24

F
Fanon, Franz, 50
Feminist pedagogy, 13, 15, 19–22, 49, 67, 69

Focusing, 3, 14, 64–66
Foucault, Michel, 60
Freire, Paolo, 19

G
Genderfluid, 15
Gender parity, 3, 5
Generosity, 12, 14, 73, 75, 77–79, 88, 93
Genius, cult of, 13, 29, 34, 38, 39
Gilligan, Carol, 80
Gimmler, Antje, 66
Global crises, 93
Gouges, Olympe de, 44
Gournay, Mari de, 44

H
Harassment, 7–10, 14, 53, 90
Harding, Sandra, 24
Hartsock, Nancy, 24
Haug, Frigga, 20
Haynes, Patricia, 56
Hegel, G. W. F., 24
Heidegger, Martin, 37
Héloïse, 32, 44
Hierarchy, 20, 39, 74, 75, 77
Hill-Collins, Patricia, 10, 20
Hipparchia, 30–33
Historicity, 59
Homosociality, 33, 34, 89
Honneth, Axel, 78
hooks, bell, 19, 21
Hypatia, 31, 33

I
Illeris, Knud, 67
Implicit bias, 2, 10, 11, 44, 76, 90, 92
Inner speech, 35
Intersectionality, 14, 20, 68
Irigaray, Luce, 32, 40

K
Kant, Immanuel, 36, 43
Knowing
    not-knowing, 3, 56
    ownership of knowledge, 32, 51

L
Lacan, Jacques, 25

Lectures, 20, 21, 45, 65, 66, 68, 69, 77, 82, 91
Le Dœuff, Michèle, 13
Levinas, Emmanuel, 79

M
Macaulay, Catharine, 19
Marinella, Lucrezia, 33, 44
Marx, Karl, 25
Mauss, Marcel, 79
Melissa, 30, 31
Memory work, 20, 21
Meritocracy, 92, 93
Merleau-Ponty, Maurice, 35, 62
MeToo, #, 8, 14, 20
Micro-inequity, 10, 90, 92
Mills, Charles W., 56
Mindfulness, 20
Misogyny, 93
Myia, 30, 31
Mys, 30

N
Neoliberalism, 93
Nietzsche, Friedrich, 37, 38, 79
Noddings, Nel, 80
Nonbinary, 15
Nussbaum, Martha, 40

O
Opting out, 1, 5, 6, 34

P
Passion, 14, 45, 49, 78, 87
Pedagogy of liberation, 19
Perictione, 30
Pettersen, Tove, 80, 82, 88
Phenomenology, 3, 4, 7, 62, 65, 68
Phintys, 29–32, 41, 42
Plato, 19, 29–31, 40, 41, 44, 50, 51, 75, 78
Positive discrimination, 12, 13
Posthumanism, 20
Power struggles, 14, 22, 73, 76, 87
Privilege walk, 22
Problem-based learning
    project-oriented—problem-based learning, 23, 67
Psychoanalytic theory, 3
Puzzle solving, philosophy as, 61
Pythagoreans, 30, 63

R
Race, 2, 3, 5, 11, 20, 21, 40, 49, 53, 56, 59, 87, 89, 90
Recognition, 3, 32, 35, 39, 52, 73, 78, 79
Reflectivity, 76
Remote learning, 15, 62
Reuter, Martina, 44
Roland, Madame, 44
Rousseau, Jean-Jacques, 44, 45

S
Sartre, Jean-Paul, 24
Schopenhauer, Arthur, 37, 38
Seminars, 37, 45, 55, 61–63, 66, 75
Senses, 3, 14, 24, 25, 39, 41, 42, 49–51, 53, 54, 61, 62, 64, 65, 67, 76, 80, 82, 88, 89
Sexual orientation, 2, 3, 21, 49, 56
Situation, 2–5, 7, 8, 10, 11, 13–15, 19–24, 29, 33, 34, 37, 40, 45, 49, 53–58, 60–62, 73, 74, 76–79, 81, 88–90, 92, 93
Social class, 3, 21, 49, 83, 87
Socrates, 30, 31, 39, 41, 75

Sound walk, 62
Stereotype threat, 2, 10, 11, 90, 92
Summer school, 4, 13, 14, 19, 21, 23, 29, 44–46, 49, 63–68, 73, 81–83, 88

T
Theano, 30
Thorgeirsdottir, Sigridur, 64
Transgender, 10
Trigger warning, 21, 91
Tronto, Joan, 80
Tyranny, 80

U
Underrepresentation, 1, 2, 4, 7, 11, 13, 14, 56, 58, 87, 89

W
Wittgenstein, Ludwig, 38
Wollstonecraft, Mary, 19, 43, 45
Wright, Richard, 24

The manufacturer's authorised representative in the EU is Springer Nature Customer Service Centre GmbH, Europaplatz 3, 69115 Heidelberg, Germany. If you have any concerns regarding our products, please contact ProductSafety@springernature.com

Printed and bound by CPI Group (UK) Ltd, Croydon, CR0 4YY

23/03/2026
02076395-0017